A Bite-Sized Public Af

Carmageddon?

Brexit & Beyond for UK Auto

Edited by
David Bailey, Alex De Ruyter, Neil Fowler and John Mair

Published by Bite-Sized Books Ltd 2020

Bite-Sized Books Ltd Cleeve Croft, Cleeve Road, Goring RG8 9BJ UK
information@bite-sizedbooks.com
Registered in the UK. Company Registration No: 9395379

Bite-Sized Books Ltd Cleeve Croft, Cleeve Road, Goring RG8 9BJ UK
information@bite-sizedbooks.com
Registered in the UK. Company Registration No: 9395379
ISBN: 9798600238367

Contents

Acknowledgments

This book could not be more timely; 2019 saw a 'perfect storm' hit UK auto, and the UK now prepares to exit the EU with many issues – such as over the nature of the future trading relationship – still to be resolved."

It is the second edition of the third in the Bite-Sized Brexit series – the first edition being *Keeping the Wheels on the Road*. The series has been steered by Paul Davies, and it was possible thanks to the editors, their contacts and their specialist knowledge. The authors, as ever writing for free (as do the editors), make the book what it is.

David Bailey wishes to acknowledge the support of the Economic and Social Research Council's *UK in a Changing Europe programme*, Grant Reference: ES/T000848/1 for his chapter in this volume.

We are very grateful to all of them and hope this informs the public debate, which is still in the midst of a long journey.

David Bailey, Birmingham
Alex De Ruyter, Birmingham (and Australia)
Neil Fowler, Northumberland
John Mair, Oxford

The Editors

David Bailey is Professor of Business Economics at the Birmingham Business School, University of Birmingham, UK and an ESRC *UK in a Changing Europe Senior Fellow.* He has written extensively on industrial and regional policy, especially in relation to manufacturing and the auto industry. He has been involved in a number of recent major projects including the Horizon2020 Rise project Makers where he led the work package on industrial policy. He is Editor-in-Chief of the leading journal *Regional Studies* and chair of the *RSA Europe* think tank and policy forum. David is a regular media commenter and newspaper columnist. Tweet him @dgbailey

Alex de Ruyter is a professor at Birmingham City University and serves as Director of its Centre for Brexit Studies. He brings a wealth of research experience and academic engagement in the areas of globalisation, regional economic development, labour market and social exclusion issues. He has published more than 60 academic outputs in leading national and international economic journals and has been the recipient of research funding, including being an investigator in an ESRC funded study on the effects on subsequent employment experience of workers from MG Rover after plant closure in 2005.

He has undertaken numerous media interviews and is currently researching on the likely impact of Brexit on the UK automotive supply chain in addition to exploring working in the 'gig economy'. He is also a Board member of the Regional Studies Association.

Neil Fowler has been in journalism since graduation, starting life as trainee reporter on the *Leicester Mercury*. He went on to edit four regional dailies, including *The Journal* in the north east of England and *The Western Mail* in Wales. He was then publisher of *The Toronto Sun* in Canada before returning to the UK to edit *Which?* magazine. In 2010/11 he was the Guardian Research Fellow at Oxford University's Nuffield College where he investigated the decline and future of regional and local newspapers in the UK. He remains an Associate Member of Nuffield and now acts as an adviser to organisations on their management and their external and internal communications and media policies and strategies.

John Mair has taught journalism at the Universities of Coventry, Kent, Northampton, Brunel, Edinburgh Napier, Guyana and the Communication University of China. He has edited 28 'hackademic' volumes over the last eight years on subjects ranging from trust in television, the health of investigative journalism, reporting the 'Arab Spring', to three volumes on the Leveson Inquiry. John also created the Coventry Conversations, which attracted 350 media movers and shakers to Coventry University. Since then, he has launched the Northampton Chronicles, Media Mondays at Napier and most recently the Harrow Conversations at Westminster University. In a previous life, he was an award-winning producer/director for the BBC, ITV and Channel 4, and a secondary school teacher.

Foreword

An industry once with bright hopes now facing an uncertain future

Sir Vince Cable

The auto industry in the UK pre-2016 was a remarkable success story with high levels of investment and output growth, and its success underpinned by a number of key factors.

The first was close industry collaboration with government, started by Peter Mandelson and then developed by myself in my time as Business Secretary, through the work of the Automotive Council and a collaborative industrial policy.

The second was the ability of UK plants to win contracts for new models thanks in large part to frictionless trade with the (rest of the) EU by being part of the EU customs union and single market, as well as huge efforts by government, management and workers to win new contracts. Indeed, as the Society of Motor Manufacturers and Traders (SMMT) had noted, annual output was on track to reach two million vehicles by 2020.

This now seems like a distant dream. Indeed, UK government spokespersons are already talking about automobiles being a declining industry, which was the language of the 1970s before Japanese investment showed the capacity for regeneration through new technology and good management systems.

Similar potential exists today, but rather, Brexit now threatens to undo the frictionless trade that underpinned supply chains that extended deep into Europe, and so the viability of UK auto assembly.

In this context, at this late juncture we still don't – remarkably – know what form Brexit will actually take. Will it really be a 'bare-bones' Canada-style free-trade agreement that would look to eliminate tariffs for manufacturers but leave us outside of the single market and therefore subject to non-tariff barriers, which could disrupt supply chains with customs delays?

Or will we exit the so-called transition period of *de facto* EU membership at the end of 2020 with no deal in place? Or will there be a Swiss-style series of sectoral agreements in place, which might anchor the auto industry in the UK?

Transition in place

Amidst this, the wider changes facing the industry, with autonomous, connected and electric vehicles coming to the fore mean that UK auto need to make a major transition.

The danger is that Brexit uncertainty means that UK auto is not putting its best foot forward in attracting the investment in these new technologies. We have seen a recent example of this with Elon Musk announcing in no undramatic fashion that the UK was out of the running for the Tesla Giga Factory for making batteries and its Model 3 because of Brexit – and that he chose Berlin instead.

So the industry face big challenges on a number of fronts. A previously vibrant industry that provides high value jobs and supports much in the way of innovation, investment, R&D and exports is now at risk. Not only is the form of Brexit critical for its future but so too is a renewed effort in terms of industrial policy to seize the opportunities from the transition to electric vehicles.

As such, I am pleased to introduce this book, which brings together leading contributors from academia, industry and public policy.

About the contributor

Sir Vince Cable was the Liberal Democratic Secretary of State for Business, Innovation and Skills in the UK coalition government of 2010-2015.

Introduction

On the road but going where?

David Bailey and Neil Fowler

The UK car industry is in crisis as **Sir Vince Cable** highlights in the foreword of this book. There can be no doubt about that. But the exact causes are a matter of intense debate. Is it a perfect storm of diesel phobia, electric adulation, urban congestion and millennial minimalism that has led to a sudden downturn in our near century-long love affair with the motor car?

And is Brexit the final factor that has come along to confirm that all is troubling the automotive world? Or is Brexit, and the uncertainty that has prevailed over the past three years or so around it, the principal cause of this current malaise?

This book seeks to explore the underlying elements that have created this maelstrom – and the contributors offer real and often opposing insights in to what has been happening and where the sector may end up.

Justin Cox and **David Oakley** of *LMC Automotive* start us off by forensically analysing the statistics – which don't make for pretty reading. They are pessimistic on what may happen in the event of no deal at the end of 2020: "It would be overly optimistic to assume that manufacturers which export large portions of their UK output to the EU would continue to do so indefinitely under persistently unprofitable operating conditions" they say.

"Indeed, should more of these currently UK-produced models fail to be renewed in Britain, annual UK car production could be over 500,000 units lower in the second half of the next decade when compared with our base view."

Ross Clark is much more optimistic, though he is scathing on the failings of big auto companies: "When Nissan announced in 2019 that it would not, after all, produce its new X-Trail in Sunderland, this was reported as proof of an impending Brexit disaster. A Labour councillor in South Wales even suggested that 'all those who voted to leave should be laid off first'. But Nissan's decision had little to do with Brexit, and everything to do with the turmoil of the global car industry" he writes.

"It is not that overall car sales are plunging — they grew by a modest 0.5 per cent across Europe in 2018 and 1.3 per cent in 2019. The problem is that established carmakers have failed to keep up, and their future now looks far more uncertain than it did even just a few years ago."

Ian Henry of *AutoAnalysis* is another who has delved in to the figures and who has been listening to what some outsiders have been saying. "Before the Brexit referendum was even a gleam in David Cameron's eye, UK car production was heading towards 2m units a year. Now it is running at around 1.3m units a year, with the risk of output falling below 1m a year.

"Of course, the decline in UK output is not entirely due to Brexit, as the diesel issue, problems in China and disappointing sales of many UK-made models have all contributed to the decline in production.

"However, Brexit's cost and practical impacts should not be underestimated. Additional production costs of £3bn a year and £8bn a year in lost economic value creation are sums which any industry would struggle to bear unscathed. Given the global headwinds battering UK vehicle production, we can expect further major challenges for this once thriving, but now troubled, sector.

Leading economist **Vicky Pryce** agrees that the automotive sector is braced for a rough time ahead. She notes that "a longer transition period beyond December 2020 would help, but there is no guarantee that this will be on the table. What will emerge after the UK leaves remains unclear. And then there is the question of financial support. Will the sums of money that are currently earmarked for transport, including the automotive sector, under the Horizon 2020 budget agreement and the Horizon Europe that succeeds it, still flow to UK car manufacturing?

She adds that "high levels of cross border research and development have been important in assisting competitiveness in the sector. In early January 2020 it was suggested that the new government's appetite to spend more supporting industry, R&D and the regions on the back of relaxed fiscal rules, while borrowing costs remained at their current near record low levels, might provide some relief."

"But for the sector in the end much will depend on what type of trade agreement we strike with the EU. Will we get there? And what is more, will we get there in a year which seems to be the new deadline when the transition period is due to come to an end? Don't hold your breath."

Hamid Moradlou, Hendrik Reefke and **Heather Skipworth** offer interesting insights on how Brexit has shaped corporate decision-making processes regarding the location of supply chain activities, noting that "for the first time in more than 40 years, manufacturers and distributors have had to contemplate tariff barriers, non-tariff barriers, and the fundamentals of market access in their UK-EU trade deliberations".

They note that one consequence "is that some manufacturing activity is likely to move offshore, away from the UK and to the EU. Equally clearly, companies serving the UK directly from the EU are likely to invest in UK-based distribution centres and inventory holdings. In both cases, the overall consequence is likely to be some erosion of manufacturing economies of scale, due to increased production fragmentation, and lower levels of inventory turn."

They add that in contrast to economic theory "the relative cost of labour and the relative cost of production appeared to have little influence on the EU-UK location decision. Instead it is issues such as market access, trade frictions, and potential tariffs that are seen as more important."

Tom Leeson of *OpenText* also reflects on research on how the UK's automotive industry has been preparing for Brexit, identifying the likely implications that different Brexit options could have on the industry in five key business areas: supply chain management; operations and logistics; human resource management; regulations and compliance; and customer communications.

He sets out a number of key recommendations about how, deal or no deal, automotive companies could prepare for Brexit, and notes that "like all manufacturing industries, the automotive sector face a gauntlet of challenges and success is largely contingent upon being able to adapt and overcome".

He notes that the digital imperative "with the industry entering into a time of significant change and disruption, automakers will need to deploy digital transformation solutions to increase the efficient of their business and to be competitive. The same solutions could help address many of the challenges posed by Brexit by streamlining and automating business processes, so making a business more agile and robust through better information utilisation that saves time and money.

He stresses that often "justification in such investment requires a compelling event to trigger change. As one of the biggest events in economic history – for the UK, EU and beyond – Brexit is such a compelling event".

Another long term industry observer, **Neil Winton**, takes a more positive view of prospects for the industry than many, echoing the chapter by Ross Clark: "Experts say there will be big challenges for the auto industry outside of the EU, but it should thrive nonetheless. Any free-trade deal with the EU will be relatively easy because it really amounts to simply consolidating what already exists" he says.

"The industry will have to raise productivity because it will no longer be able to hide behind the 10 per cent tariff barrier provided by the EU. The industry won't welcome having to improve efficiency but the likes of Jaguar Land Rover (JLR) already manage to do this very successfully. Now they will be able to source components not just from the EU but also the rest of the world".

Winton notes however that "the free-trade deal with Japan raises the question about whether Toyota and Nissan would want to remain in the UK even if it were firmly in the EU for the long term. It's unlikely in the short term that these companies would want to shut down very efficient factories because big global manufacturers need to insure themselves against things like exchange rate fluctuations and perhaps tariff wars too. Having a paid-for alternative makes good business sense."

David Bailey is rather more sceptical, stressing that the form of trade deal done with the EU will still be critical: "While no deal is seen by many in industry as highly damaging, even a limited trade deal that simply eliminates most tariffs – of the sort envisaged in the latest political declaration – could still cause severe headaches for industry given issues of regulatory divergence and through the UK being outside the EU customs union," he says.

He goes on to suggest that this "means another year of uncertainty for big auto assemblers, which in turn means that it is unlikely that we see any immediate bounce back in investment in UK automotive and manufacturing".

Bailey argues that "'taking back control' means the ability for the UK to set new regulations and standards after Brexit but the knock-on effect will likely mean more customs checks and possible delays to, say, manufacturing components moving across borders, bringing challenges for manufacturers."

He stresses that "to eliminate border bureaucracy there would need to be an FTA (free-trade agreement) arrangement and some sort of mutual recognition agreement for assessing conformity assessment... However, to ensure automatic mutual recognition of the UK's conformity assessment, European Economic Area (EEA) states have to accept supranational enforcement. This could violate a UK 'red line' in Brexit talks."

Next **Ben Norman** and **Steve Turner** of the union Unite report the findings of new research on how Brexit is impacting in the workplace, based on interviews with frontline workplace reps across industries, supported by polling of 2,000 automotive workers.

They note that the results showed that "Brexit uncertainty had affected almost all the interviewed reps, with 60 per cent reporting at least one workplace issue linked to Brexit. While 10 per cent reported a direct impact, such as a postponement of new investment, 34 per cent believed that their employer was making a virtue of a crisis to use Brexit opportunistically at the bargaining table."

They go on to say that "this uncertainty fed into a deepening 'Brexit fatigue' across workplaces, which in turn exasperated divisions wrought by the referendum in 2016. Importantly, the research showed that 60 per cent of workplace reps have taken the initiative industrially to restore certainty, fend off any cases of opportunism and begin healing difficult political divisions."

This has been done with some employers, "where collective bargaining is strong and relationships have developed, most notably in the automotive sector, this has meant using information and consultation agreements or European Works Councils to secure a seat at the table to participate in Brexit contingency planning or to use pay talks to negotiate commitments to protect working rights in collective agreements. With a (significant) minority of employers, this meant using the collective strength of the membership to face down opportunistic attacks on pay or our bargaining rights."

The book concludes with a sobering perspective from Australia, written by co-editor **Alex De Ruyter**. His key point is that no country has a right to having a car industry. In 1970 the country was producing some 475,000 cars a year, he writes. But from then on, for various reasons, decline set in. "By the end of 2017 a period of some 70 years of large-scale vehicle production in Australia had come to an end", he says.

"For the Brexiting Britain, the parallels are striking. Like Australia in its protectionist days, domestic production was feasible when the presence of external trade barriers acted as an inhibitor to exporting to the UK from a country of origin outside the EU; and the location-specific advantages of the UK with its flexible market environment *inside* the EU made it an attractive location to be a production platform integrated with the rest of the EU.

"Stripped of these advantages post-Brexit and facing likely new tariff and regulatory barriers, the clear incentive – as Honda and Nissan are currently demonstrating – for multinationals, will be to divest themselves over the coming period of production in the UK and reinvest elsewhere."

Chapter 1

Overt optimism cannot hide the facts

2020 vision? The macro impact on the auto sector could still be devastating, say Justin Cox and David Oakley of LMC Automotive

As we write, the terms of the UK's future relationship with the EU post-2020 are still highly uncertain. With the UK formally leaving the EU on January 31 this year and entering a transition period until the end of the year, the nature of the longer-term trading relationship is not yet known.

The possibilities include the UK reverting to trading on World Trade Organisation (WTO) rules if no trade deal can be struck this year – henceforth referred to as a no-deal Brexit – and a 'bare bones' trade deal, eliminating tariffs.

There is the possibility of an extended transition period beyond December 2020, with the aim of a comprehensive free-trade agreement following, though any delay would be something of a U-turn by prime minister Boris Johnson. The Conservative government, now bolstered by a strong majority in parliament, has indicated that it is keen to diverge from EU standards in some areas, raising the possibility that the future arrangements will be somewhat closer to the 'harder' Brexit scenarios, even if a trade deal is agreed in a timely manner.

As ever with Brexit, though, it is difficult to be certain how much of the debate on all sides is intended as a negotiating tactic rather than a serious long-term strategy.

Remarkably then, as we head towards the four-year anniversary of the referendum, the UK's future trading relationship with the EU is still unclear. As the transition period extends all current trade arrangements to the end of 2020, we assume no macroeconomic impact at the time of the technical Brexit date of January 31.

Beyond 2020

The likelihood of the UK government achieving its aim of completing a free-trade agreement with the EU by the end of 2020 looks ambitious and a transition period extending to the end of 2022 appears more realistic, despite UK government insistence this can be wrapped up sooner.

Our partner Oxford Economics (OE) sees UK GDP growth at an average of 1.5 per cent in 2020-22. The relatively positive medium-term forecast reflects fiscal loosening from the Treasury as well as a boost from pent-up demand due to the uncertainty created by Brexit.

Away from the base case, the risk of no deal still looms. Under a no-deal scenario, OE is not forecasting that the UK enters a prolonged recession, although two consecutive quarters of negative growth can be expected, with no deal acting as a drag to the tune of up to 1-1.5 percentage points per year. The worst potential effects of no deal would be mitigated, OE assumes, by higher government spending – and therefore a greater tolerance for a higher deficit, at least temporarily – as well as a cut in interest rates, to 0.25 per cent. This interest rate cut would be delivered despite a spike in CPI inflation.

The impact on sales

UK light vehicle (LV) sales – which include both personal vehicles and light commercial vehicles – totalled 2.73m units in 2018 and 2.68m in 2019. While these represent ongoing falls year-on-year, it should be noted that the UK market is receding from an all-time record of 3.08m units in 2016, and a cyclical slowdown would anyway be expected. In addition, Brexit is certainly not the only factor that has been affecting sales in recent times, although uncertainty around the future of the economy is seen as a cause of slowing sales as 2018 and 2019 progressed.

The introduction of a new emissions testing procedure, known as WLTP, disrupted sales across Europe back in 2018, with sales still struggling to fully recover by year-end. Furthermore, diesel sales have declined severely amidst a spate of negative publicity for the fuel type, linked to harmful emissions and therefore potential bans in the future. With some, more modest, WLTP disruption in 2019 and continuing low levels of consumer and business confidence, vehicle sales contracted once again.

Under our baseline outlook, we assume an orderly exit from the EU with a trade deal post-2022 in place. LV sales are on a weak footing and with GDP slowing once again in 2020, we forecast sales falling a little over 1 per cent this year, before returning to modest growth of circa 2 per cent in 2021, by which time LV sales will be 2.7m.

However, under a no-deal scenario, a number of macroeconomic factors would conspire to put downward pressure on sales. As well as a reduction in GDP growth, the pound would depreciate sharply, by – OE expects – almost 15 per cent on a trade-weighted basis. This would increase the cost of vehicles in the UK, given that most cars sold in the UK are imported (predominantly from the EU), and even those that are locally manufactured rely on international supply chains. Add to this, a 10 per cent WTO tariff to be applied on the imported vehicles, and the pressure on prices begins to really accumulate.

Supply chains would also be affected by 10 per cent tariffs in the event of a no deal, as well as non-tariff barriers such as increased customs checks at the border, all of which will increase cost pressures on manufacturers.

The effect of sterling's fall

After sterling's depreciation in the wake of the 2016 referendum, automakers absorbed some of the costs stemming from the weaker pound, but would surely struggle to do so much further were the currency to slip to the levels predicted by OE, and tariffs were applied. For example, it was recently reported that Brexit disclaimers are being applied to invoices for imported vehicles such that the customer absorbs any tariff-related price increase prior to vehicle delivery, thereby protecting company margins.

We expect that the combined impact of these effects (sterling falling, tariffs, macroeconomic weakness) would be to reduce UK LV sales by around 12 per cent compared to the baseline scenario for 2021, with a market outturn of 2.38m against the base case of 2.70m sales. Over the 2020 to 2024 period, we forecast that a cumulative 1m UK sales could be lost in a no-deal scenario, versus the base case.

The impact on production

Although the effect on other countries would be much less significant, we still see global sales being reduced by some 300,000 units per year in the near-term, in addition to those lost in the UK, if no deal is agreed.

The auto industries in the UK and Europe are closely integrated. Common regulatory EU-wide frameworks have evolved to facilitate the development of highly complex automotive supply chains, which now underpin a business model that relies on just-in-time and just-in-sequence delivery and production.

This business model will be affected by Brexit, but the scale of impact depends on which scenario is pursued: our base transitional Brexit or the no-deal scenario.

The UK is estimated to have produced 1.42m light vehicles in 2019 and, of this total, almost 80 per cent were exported globally, with the EU receiving more than 55 per cent of this volume. However, it is important to appreciate the complexity of automotive manufacturing with each finished vehicle consisting of thousands of components, which in turn are processed and traded across multiple borders. For UK production, 44 per cent of a vehicle's content is sourced locally, with almost 80 per cent of the remaining non-domestic content coming from the EU.

In a no-deal Brexit, barrier-free access to the EU market is expected to end with the UK withdrawing from the EU on WTO terms. Under these terms, a 10 per cent tariff would be applied to all traded goods. Coupled with regulatory requirements, these new customs procedures will inevitably add barriers to trade, increase red-tape and ultimately cost. Border checks in particular will cause delays and undermine the efficiency of the just-in-time model.

Although the threat of an imminent no-deal Brexit has dissipated following the UK government's agreement to enter the transitional EU-withdrawal phase, the shape of Brexit beyond 2020, at the end of transition, remains unclear. Indeed, without sufficient trade negotiation progress being made, the automotive industry may well still face another cliff-edge moment at the end of 2020 as the prospects of a no-deal Brexit reappear.

In this situation, we could see year-end contingency stock-building provide a modest 1.5 per cent boost to the UK's 2020 LV production outlook, when measured against our current base-case view. However, the impact of a no-deal Brexit would begin to fall heavily in 2021 as unwinding of stocks, weaker competitiveness and a falling domestic market combine to undermine the UK's LV production volume: we expect output could fall below 1.4m units – 10 per cent lower than our current base-case view.

Investment may go to the EU

Longer term, continuing obstacles to trade associated with a no-deal Brexit may encourage an increase in UK component manufacturing onshoring. However, fears persist that UK domestic original equipment manufacturers (OEMs) lack the required local market scale to attract investment by key volume component suppliers – very simply, large capacity investment decisions are more likely to gravitate to the EU where the combined potential of the single market offers the greatest volume opportunity and manufacturing economies. This is particularly relevant for an industry which is facing such technological change as all automakers grapple with huge new investment decisions required to accommodate the evolution of electrification and autonomous driving.

For UK-based OEMs, a no-deal Brexit might even threaten the existence of certain assembly facilities. Indeed, the fear of a no-deal scenario may have contributed to the announcements by Nissan to cancel the expansion plans of its Sunderland plant, and Honda, which has confirmed that it will close its UK manufacturing operation in Swindon from 2021.

Admittedly, much of these decisions are based upon the new EU-Japan trading accord. In force since February 2019, this new trade agreement ensures that the EU's 10 per cent tariff on Japanese auto imports will be tapered to zero over the next ten years.

Increasingly Japanese OEMs may choose to import new models rather than invest and continue to localise production in their European transplants. For the UK, whose access to the EU's single market originally attracted Japanese automakers, Brexit adds another dimension. Should the UK leave without a deal and WTO tariffs are applied to UK vehicle exports, the same cars made in Japan may well end up costing less to import into the EU27 than those produced just across the Channel in Britain.

With the UK's Japanese transplants collectively producing almost half of the UK's LV output in 2019, and Toyota and Nissan respectively exporting 79 per cent and 60 per cent of their production to the EU, risks for further industrial shrinkage are significant.

For PSA Group, which is battling with overcapacity, the Opel/Vauxhall Ellesmere Port plant may be tough to justify after 2021, when the current-generation Astra compact model produced there is slated for replacement. Peugeot has already issued a clear warning on possibly shifting Astra production to southern Europe in the event of no deal. Jaguar Land Rover, meanwhile, could divert more production to a new facility in Slovakia and/or increase contract production with Magna in Austria.

As a result, it would be overly optimistic to assume that manufacturers which export large portions of their UK output to the EU would continue to do so indefinitely under persistently unprofitable operating conditions. Indeed, should more of these currently UK-produced models fail to be renewed in Britain, annual UK car production could be over 500,000 units lower in the second half of the next decade when compared with our base view.

About the contributors

Justin Cox is Director, Global Production, at LMC Automotive. In this role he provides the functional lead and global oversight of the company's automotive production forecast activity. With more than 20 years of extensive automotive business experience, including OEM and supplier roles, he has gained a 'real-world' insight into the commercial pressures and planning challenges facing the industry throughout the value-chain. Justin holds a BSc degree in Economics and Human Geography from the University of Reading.

David Oakley is an analyst at LMC Automotive. His role has included LV sales forecasting for the Middle East and Africa, selected markets across Western and Eastern Europe, and more recently North America. He holds a First-Class degree in Politics from the University of Nottingham, and enjoys applying political and economic analysis to the automotive industry.

LMC Automotive is the leading independent and exclusively automotive focused provider of global forecasting and market intelligence in the areas of vehicle sales, production, powertrains and electrification. Highly respected for its responsive customer support, the company's client base from around the globe includes car and truck makers, component manufacturers and suppliers, financial, logistics and government institutions.

Chapter 2

The auto industry struggling in a changing world

The motor giants are facing a challenging future which has little to do with Brexit, says Ross Clark

When Nissan announced in 2019 that it would not, after all, produce its new X-Trail in Sunderland, this was reported as proof of an impending Brexit disaster. A Labour councillor in South Wales even suggested that 'all those who voted to leave should be laid off first'. But Nissan's decision had little to do with Brexit, and everything to do with the turmoil of the global car industry.

It is not that overall car sales are plunging — they grew by a modest 0.5 per cent across Europe in 2018 and 1.3 per cent in 2019. The problem is that established carmakers have failed to keep up, and their future now looks far more uncertain than it did even just a few years ago.

BMW, Mercedes, Volkswagen, Nissan: for decades, the same names ruled. It was a complacent industry, and progress was incremental. Every five years or so, a new model of car would be brought out that was slightly better, slightly more efficient than the last. The domination of the internal combustion engine meant that this piece of late 19th-century technology set a huge entry barrier to new entrants. You couldn't set up a car company from scratch and hope to steal a march on the established players.

Upstarts upset the market

So they scoffed at suggestions that their world might be upended by electronic cars, ride-sharing apps like Uber — which could mean fewer people owning cars — or various degrees of driverless technology.

But life has come at them hard. Tesla has proved that there is a large market (and long waiting lists) for premium electric models — and, so far, the company has defied the short-sellers who have bet on its demise. As for self-driving technology, it is Google which has led the way, investing more than a billion dollars. A fatal accident in 2018 hasn't deterred Uber either. Eager to catch up, Toyota invested $500m in Uber in the same year to help develop self-driving technology.

Driverless technology is crucial for the future shape of the automotive sector because it promises to slash the cost of taking a taxi — which could undermine car ownership altogether, at least in cities.

The established car industry knows it will have to move away from petrol and diesel, but is unsure in which technology to invest. Electric cars have been touted as the future but, alternatively, it may turn out that hydrogen fuel cells prove to be the low-emission, carbon-neutral long-term replacement for petrol and diesel. Toyota is certainly looking that way — it recently launched a hydrogen car, the Mirai. Hyundai, too, is investing heavily in hydrogen, last December announcing a £5.5bn investment in the technology The battle between the two — hydrogen vs electric — has been dubbed by analysts at KPMG the car industry's 'Betamax vs VHS' moment, echoing the big battle over video technology in the 1980s.

Electric cars ought to be more efficient, as hydrogen first has to be extracted from water — there being no natural earthly source for pure hydrogen. But then, unlike battery cars, hydrogen cells can be refuelled in minutes. That is one reason why, according to a survey by KPMG, motor executives believe battery cars will eventually lose the battle. But nobody knows, which is what makes the future so uncertain for the car industry. And we all know how the video battle played out — a victory for VHS before it, in turn, was blown away by DVD.

Governments killing off the diesel
But the bigger factor in the car giants' malaise is the way governments have sought to speed up the car revolution by killing off traditional engines. What did for the Sunderland X-Trail — a big, bad diesel car — was not Brexit but Michael Gove's announcement in July 2017, echoed in France, that all new diesel and petrol cars will be banned from 2040. Then came initiatives like London's Ultra-Low Emissions zone, which from April

2019 has imposed new charges on older diesel vehicles entering the congestion charge zone.

You can see versions of this all over the western world. A recent German court ruling allowed cities to ban diesel cars completely. With restrictions in Belgium and the Netherlands too, motorists are becoming reluctant to buy them. On top of this, Nissan had been struggling to make its diesel X-Trail compliant with the latest EU emissions regulations. When the company made its pledge in 2016, things looked very different than they do now.

The technology now on the way — be it battery, hydrogen cell or something else — is not necessarily going to be developed by the old players. Meanwhile, the old companies are being shaken by scandal. Martin Winterkorn had to quit as chairman of Volkswagen after the company was found to have cheated in emissions tests when it was struggling to develop cleaner engines. In elate 2018, BMW was fined $10m over its handling of a spate of engine fires in South Korea. Carlos Ghosn, the Nissan chief executive who made the decision to build the X-Trail in Sunderland, is currently on charges for fraud, and the company is to be run by a more Japan-centric management.

Cities are also becoming hostile environments for cars — with congestion charges and ever-tighter parking restrictions. It's not that cars will disappear — but in future, urbanites will be far less likely to own them and more likely to hire them on an intermittent basis. While the number of UK residents with a driving licence continues to creep upwards, there has been a huge shift in the age profile over the past quarter century. In 1994, half of 17- to 20-year-olds could drive; now it's less than a third. How many of the Uber generation will ever own a car? No one knows, but if you are a car manufacturer whose business model assumes the continued growth of what Mrs Thatcher liked to call 'the great car economy', with two cars on the driveway of the archetypal middle-class home, it is enough to put your strategy in a spin.

Factories closing around the world
As manufacturers wrestle with the consequences of these various trends, factories are closing at an increasing rate. GM closed five plants across the US and one in Canada in 2019 as it sought to invest more in electric

vehicles. Ford cut 1,600 jobs in Germany as it, too, sought to invest more in electric cars. The people of Sunderland — where, by the way, Nissan is not proposing to cut a single job, only to cancel a planned expansion of its existing plant — are the lucky ones. Nissan's factory there is one of the most efficient in the world and not so long ago was producing more cars than the whole of Italy.

No one yet knows who the winners of Carmageddon will be, but for the moment initiative seems to be slipping away eastwards. China, until recently damned as the dirty man of the world for its fondness for opening new coal-fired power stations, has taken to electric vehicles with an enthusiasm greater than anywhere else. In 2018, the Chinese bought a million electric cars, a 60 per cent increase in two years — this in spite of an overall fall in car sales in the country.

Western luxury carmakers, who for years have relied on selling their products to a fast-expanding Chinese middle class, are suddenly looking flat-footed. It was principally falling Chinese demand which led Jaguar Land Rover to announce last year that it is chopping 5,000, or one in eight, UK jobs — although inevitably that too was mistakenly interpreted as a consequence of Brexit.

It is easy to exaggerate trends. While diesel sales are in steep decline, electric vehicles still account for no more than 2 per cent of new vehicle registrations in most European countries (Norway, on nearly 40 per cent, is an outlier). By some estimates, at the end of the next decade, one in five cars bought in America will be electric. But for the moment, it is petrol and petrol hybrids which are filling the gap as consumers turn away from diesel (sales of which were down 22 per cent in the UK in 2019, while petrol sales rose 2 per cent).

Battery technology is developing fast, and the price of the batteries falling fast, but it may never advance to the stage where electric cars are a viable alternative to petrol and diesel for long journeys in remote areas. And Emmanuel Macron has learnt the hard way what happens to politicians who get too carried away with green taxes: the rise of the GILETS JAUNES has shown the hazards of unleashing policies designed around the needs of cities on to rural populations, for whom, for the moment, old-fashioned cars provide the sole means of practical transport.

A head start for Sunderland

But if the electric car is to be part of the future, Nissan and Sunderland have a head start, because for several years they have been making the world's number one electric car for the mass market, the Leaf — a vehicle whose development was championed by the fallen Carlos Ghosn.

The environmentally conscious would surely prefer this vehicle to be made in Britain in place of the X-Trail. Other carmakers are now rushing to catch up: Volkswagen is in the midst of a five-year spending spree of $40bn to electrify its 300-odd models.

There is no guarantee that either Nissan or its Sunderland plant will be around in 20 years. Today's electric vehicles may by then be museum pieces, driven out by hydrogen or something we have yet to discover. But whatever technology does come to take over the car market, you can be sure that it will have been developed in an economy that supports innovation, and which has the lowest possible barriers to hiring the required talent from around the world.

So in that sense, the Nissan story IS related to Brexit. It's a reminder that the world economy is fast changing — and that success will go to whoever can step up a gear.

About the contributor

Ross Clark is a freelance journalist. An earlier version of this chapter first appeared as an article in *The Spectator*.

Chapter 3

There may be trouble ahead...

Leaving the EU with no deal would increase the automotive industry's costs significantly, by more than £3bn a year through tariffs alone; further costs would arise through non-tariff barriers and other general disruption. Ian Henry of AutoAnalysis looks at the potential dramatic effects of Brexit for UK vehicle production

Car production in the UK for the 11 months to November 2019 was just over 1.23m units[1], a fall of 14.5 per cent year-on-year. The full year figures (due out at the same time as this book was published) will likely be around 1.32m.

The November fall was actually 16.5 per cent, due in part to scheduled shutdowns at some vehicle plants in anticipation of the UK leaving the EU without a deal on October 31.

Disappointing sales of old models and planned model changeovers (e.g. the Nissan Juke switch to a new model led to zero output for several months in 2019) did not help the production environment last year. As well as declining production volumes, the vehicle manufacturing sector had – according to the Society of Motor Manufacturers and Traders SMMT – borne Brexit-related costs and contingency measures valued at more than £500m. Such is the economic cost, so far, of Brexit, and it had not even been done by November.

Brexit will, however, soon be 'done', at least in the sense of the UK legally leaving the EU's institutions. Following the Conservatives' general election victory – barring any unforeseen, last minute turn-of-events – the UK will leave the EU on January 31, 2020. It will then enter the transition period which is due to last until December 31, 2020. Unless this is extended by agreement, the UK's departure from the EU will be complete.

What happens in 2021?

The crucial issue for the automotive manufacturing sector is what will be trading environment come January 1, 2021.

This is due to be negotiated during the transition, but negotiations are unlikely to start before March and would need to be complete by October to stand a chance of being ratified by the end of the year. In terms of the automotive industry, it needs to know whether there will be tariffs on exported vehicles and components? What will the regulatory environment be? And how secure or stable will be the in-bound supply chains on which UK vehicle factories depend for their just-in-time deliveries?

The UK government says it has time during 2020 to complete a comprehensive free-trade agreement, although most independent trade policy analysts – and the EU – say this is impractical. A 'bare bones' free trade agreement is said to be possible, but what this would entail and how it would affect the automotive sector is unknown.

What we can be sure of is that in the absence of a zero tariff, zero quota and technological alignment agreement, the UK's vehicle manufacturing sector will face additional costs. Its basic economic model will be undermined; and for vehicles sold in the most price-competitive segments, these additional costs risk sending the programmes concerned into a downward spiral from which recovery may be impractical.

In the corresponding chapter in the first edition of this book, we explained that the costs of tariffs for UK exports would be around £3bn a year. The actual costs will vary with production volumes achieved and whether European consumers continue to buy UK vehicles if import tariffs are applied, and whether EU factories continue to source UK-made components if they too are subject to import tariffs.

As production and exports fall – as they are likely to do with tariffs imposed – the costs borne by the industry will also fall. But this is far from good news.

Tariffs will hit demand

The real damage will come from loss of value at the factory gate. Fewer vehicles made means lower economic output – and the risk of job losses, shifts being cut, or factory futures being placed at risk.

Calculations by AutoAnalysis undertaken for the SMMT make clear the scale of this risk[2]. A hard Brexit – taken as 10 per cent tariffs applied at the port of entry on the landed price of UK-made vehicles when they arrive in the EU – would hit EU demand for UK-made vehicles.

We calculate that 1.5m vehicles would be lost from otherwise expected UK production from 2020 through to 2024; and, taking into account the different mix of vehicles involved, from Opel Astras through to Rolls Royces, the loss of economic value at the factory gate would be nearly £43bn, or more than £8bn a year on average.

This would be not far off 20 per cent of the value of vehicle production in a 'typical' pre-Brexit year. The actual impact will vary from company to company and factories, such as Vauxhall Ellesmere Port or Toyota at Burnaston, which ship the overwhelming majority of their output to the EU, will be most severely hit by the tariff burden.

By contrast, Jaguar Land Rover (JLR) and Mini, which are less than 30 per cent dependent on the EU for their exports, will be relatively less impacted by EU tariffs. Their much bigger worry would be if the US increased tariffs on vehicle imports, currently just 2.5 per cent, to a possible 25 per cent[3]. One of the many unanswered (or unknown unknown) Brexit questions is whether such a move by the US administration would impact the UK once it left the EU.

The real worry for UK vehicle production in the event of a hard Brexit, with EU tariffs levied, is whether this turns out to be a permanent situation, or merely a temporary problem, and in this case, for how long?

Government support required

Recent discussions with senior industry executives make it clear how much of the UK vehicle production sector will be uneconomic with a permanent imposition of 10 per cent tariffs on exports to the EU. In the event of tariffs being imposed, vehicle manufacturers will look for significant government support while they adjust to the new economic order. For some factories, there may be no time; for example, PSA has made it clear that its provisional decision to allocate some – but not all – of the production of the next Astra to Ellesmere Port was dependent on the nature of the Brexit deal[4]; this is widely believed to mean that tariffs would make the plant uneconomic for exporting to the EU.

Although PSA could make Ellesmere Port into a CKD plant making a range of models for the UK market, such an approach would run counter to recent industry practice. We expect that a hard Brexit from January 1, 2021 would lead to closure of the Ellesmere Port factory very speedily.

The UK is already losing the Honda plant (officially for global reasons, as opposed to Brexit) and a much reduced production line-up at Nissan (the Infiniti range has finished, and the X-Trail will not come to the UK). These programmes alone mean a minimum permanent loss to UK production of 225-250,000 vehicles a year.

The possible closure of Ellesmere Port, and with the economics of production for the other plants (especially the remaining Japanese factories) undermined, , would see UK vehicle production will fall further.

The expected negative impact and implications of Brexit are especially unfortunate given the potential which the UK vehicle manufacturing sector still has today. Despite Brexit uncertainty, the new Vivaro has gone into production at Luton (including Peugeot, Citroen and Opel versions, for export), the electric Mini is now in production at Oxford, the Aston Martin DBX SUV is in trial build in a new factory in Wales, and JLR's Castle Bromwich plant is being reconfigured to make electric vehicle (EVs), starting with the replacement for the XJ.

Before the Brexit referendum was even a gleam in David Cameron's eye, UK car production was heading towards 2m units a year. Now it is running at around 1.3m units a year, with the risk of output falling below 1m a year.

Of course, the decline in UK output is not entirely due to Brexit, as the diesel issue, problems in China and disappointing sales of many UK-made models have all contributed to the decline in production.

However, Brexit's cost and practical impacts should not be underestimated. Additional production costs of £3bn a year and £8bn a year in lost economic value creation are sums which any industry would struggle to bear unscathed. Given the global headwinds battering UK vehicle production, we can expect further major challenges for this once thriving, but now troubled, sector.

Notes

1. https://www.smmt.co.uk/2019/12/double-digit-fall-for-november-uk-car-production-as-industry-calls-for-ambitious-eu-deal/
2. https://www.smmt.co.uk/2019/11/only-ambitious-brexit-deal-will-safeguard-jobs-and-britains-green-future/
3. https://www.dw.com/en/eu-still-cautious-about-threat-of-us-car-tariffs/a-51359266
4. https://www.autocar.co.uk/car-news/industry/vauxhall-set-build-next-generation-astra-ellesmere-port

About the contributor

Ian Henry is managing director and owner of AutoAnalysis. He has more than 30 years' experience of consulting and analysis in the automotive industry, advising major car companies, suppliers, financial sector companies and government bodies in the UK and across Europe. He is a graduate of Cambridge University and has post-graduate degrees from Henley Management College and King's College, University of London. He specialises in production forecasting, supply-chain and competitor analysis. He is a regular contributor to leading automotive business media, notably www.just-auto.com, www.automotivemanufacturingsolutions.com and www.automotiveworld.com.

Chapter 4

No light at the end of the production line

Brexit causes numerous and complex problems for the UK automotive sector, says Vicky Pryce, and there appears to be no easy answer to whatever happens

The UK automotive sector has been one of the great successes of the last decade. In 2016 it accounted for some 4 per cent of the economy, employed just under 900,000 workers, had an annual turnover of some £82bn and was one of the UK's main exports with some 80 per cent of its output destined for abroad[1].

It is one of the most productive sectors of the economy, traditionally investing some £3.6bn annually though this has fallen sharply since the Brexit referendum of June 2016.

And it has been a success story overall. Output had picked up after the serious slowdown during the financial crisis with competitiveness bolstered by a weaker exchange rate and annual production rose to 1.7m cars in 2016, the highest number since the record year of 1972 when 1.9m cars left UK factories. There were some 2.7m engines built in the UK that year.

Following the EU referendum however car production fell back by 3 per cent in 2017 and by over 9 per cent in 2018 as a whole to just 1.52m passenger vehicles, with UK car exports dropping despite the devalued Brexit pound. However the Brexit uncertainty and the threat of a no-deal scenario continued through 2019 taking its toll on the economy and on the automotive sector.

It is not surprising that the sector would suffer given the impact on both supply and demand of the Brexit vote. According to calculations by the Bank of England, the National Institute for Economic and Social Research (NIESR) and also the Centre For European Reform(CER), output in the UK economy since the referendum grew some 2.5-3 per cent less than it would have done had the referendum result gone the other way if one took into account the UK's comparative position, previous trends and world trade and GDP growth over the period.

What basically happened is that as investment was held back, indicating increased uncertainty in the economy, productivity and competitiveness suffered as did overall prosperity and real living standards of the UK population. And demand generally remained subdued despite substantial monetary easing by the Bank of England since mid 2016. Following the referendum households saw a further fall in real disposable incomes for a while as inflation rose temporarily, reflecting the fall in sterling that followed the shock result.

Of course there were external factors too. The most recent period has witnessed a slowdown in the world economy as trade disputes between China and the US escalated and trade relations between the EU and the US worsened, while Germany's industrial production machinery seems to have ground to a halt. The regulatory environment on cars is evolving with much uncertainty still on what the future for diesels and electric cars might look like as environmental concerns rise.

Business and consumer optimism low

In such an environment it would indeed be expected that demand for and production of cars in the UK would be adversely affected. But Brexit can still be seen to have had a direct negative impact on the sector. The Society of Motor Manufacturers and Traders (SMMT) has referred to Brexit as 'the most significant threat to the competitiveness of the UK automotive sector in a generation'[2].

While some of the political uncertainty has now gone following the decisive Tory victory in the general election of December 2019, concern about the length of the transition period, due to end in December 2020, and the new terms of whatever trade agreement is reached with the EU may well see the demand weakness remain for some time to come – both from individual consumers and from businesses.

Investment worries

Since the referendum, and with various Brexit deadlines approaching threatening a no-deal and then being postponed, there has hardly been enough stability or confidence to invest or produce. Business investment across all sectors has fallen in many quarters.

The latest Office for National Statistics' (ONS) estimates for the third quarter of 2019 showed stagnant growth in business capital expenditure in the three months from June to September, although it was up 0.5per cent from a year earlier[3]. And business optimism has been in general decline for some time – the Q4 2018 CBI survey suggested a further sharp drop with investment intentions on buildings, new plant and machinery and also on training showing the worst quarterly performance since the financial crisis[4].

This lack of confidence was bound to also be reflected in the car industry too. Investment in the sector has been on a declining trend in the last few years. Latest data suggest that it halved in 2018 alone with the result that car manufacturers invested just £589m in the UK compared to £2.5bn in 2015[5]. In the six months to June 2019 investment pledges fell by a further 70 per cent compared to the already poor first half of 2018.

Not surprisingly, relocating activities seems to have started already. SMMT research has been suggesting for some time that a significant percentage of firms are already moving operations out of the UK and reducing headcount, as well as reviewing and actually altering logistics and other arrangements such as warehousing and stock adjustments, to be able to cope with Brexit[6].

The reason to worry of course is that the shape of the sector has changed drastically over the past few decades. All the large manufacturers producing in the UK are foreign owned. with only smaller specialists and luxury producers still mainly in British hands[7].

The big overseas companies, producing partly for the domestic market but also massively for export, can more easily adjust and move operations due to changes in the competitive environment. Their investment plans are being followed closely and Nissan UK (Japanese owned with an annual production of 500,000 units) was one of the first companies to be visited by Theresa May to reassure it on Brexit when she became Prime Minister after the referendum.

Despite the reassurances given so far, the company has shelved its investment plans for building the new X-Trail in the UK[8], partly blaming the Brexit uncertainty for its decision. Honda announced its intention to close Swindon, which was already running at half capacity, at the end of 2021 and consolidate production in Japan[9].

It still plans to keep its European headquarters in Bracknell in the UK and the company did not attribute this decision directly to Brexit. Nevertheless uncertainty as to the final deal cannot have helped[10]. This means losses of 3,500 direct jobs and a possible further loss of an equal number again down the supply chain. Swindon workers are already blaming Brexit as a reason.[11] And it is worth bearing in mind that some 40 per cent of all components in Swindon come from the EU.[12]

In mid 2019 JLR, although seeing an improvement and return to profit towards the end of its financial year, announced a record loss in its history for 2018 as a whole[13], and had already announced plans to cut 4.500 jobs, many in the UK. It had earlier worried that a no-deal Brexit would cost it an extra £1.2bn in lost profits per annum and had implemented a series of cost-cutting measures[14].

More recently however JLR, helped by the promise it seems of a £500m loan guarantee from the government, has announced plans to assemble new electric cars in the UK and the intention to produce a new Range Rover model in Solihull. Mini intends to base its new electric hatchback at its plant in Oxford.

Output impacts

But smaller component manufactures down the supply chain will remain worried, concern about the supply chain identified by the British Chambers of Commerce (BCC) as big firms adapt to Brexit is likely if anything to intensify through the coming year.

In this environment it would be expected that car production would also be affected, and this is precisely what has been seen. In response to the prevailing uncertainty a number of the large car companies shut down output for a few weeks in April 2019 to coincide with the original deadline of March 29 – which of course came and went – and that certainly affected production early on in the year.

Honda had earlier announced plans to shut Swindon, anyway, for six days after the Brexit date of March 29 in 2019 to ensure it could handle any issues with exports to the EU and also to address any concerns in relation to its imports of components post Brexit. [15]

As a result in April 2019 car production was 44 per cent down on the previous year. Toyota, BMW and Jaguar Land Rover (JLR) all implemented further planned temporary closures in November 2019 to coincide with yet another, as it happens, missed Brexit deadline, this time under new Prime Minister Boris Johnson. Output fell by 16.5 per cent that month from the levels a year earlier.

The result is that production in the sector contracted by 14.5 per cent in the 11 months to November, having shown monthly falls for 17 out of the last 18 months[16]. This has made it the worst period of decline since 2001[17].

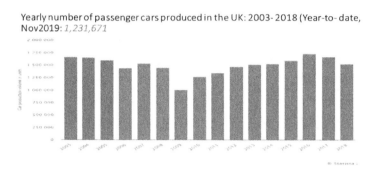

Figure 1: Car production in the UK: November 2013-2018 and October 2019 (SMMT)

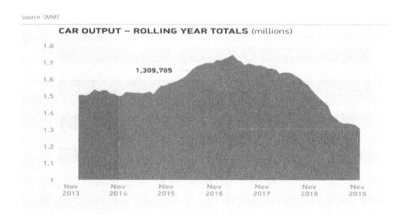

Figure 2: Rolling car output in the UK: November 2013- 2019 (SMMT)

But optimism in the sector hit the lowest in 27 years during the past year as uncertainty took its toll. And trying to cover itself against the possibility of no deal is estimated to have cost the sector some £330m in extra costs, such as extra warehousing space, stockpiling, new logistics solutions and staff training to deal with new expected customs procedures[18].

Consumer confidence

The consumer, now over-indebted again after being incentivised to borrow at record low interest, has been a major part in this slowdown.

So despite high employment rates, the fact that real wages though improving are only just getting back to the levels seen before the financial crisis, Brexit uncertainty and the lack of clarity regarding how the UK government will proceed on diesel cars have negatively affected consumer confidence in the sector impacting on car registrations.

Annual New Car Registrations

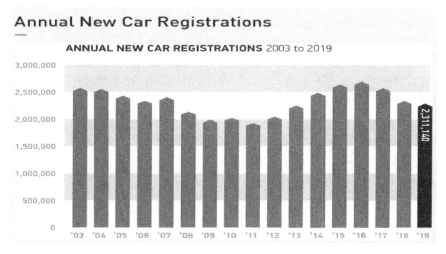

Figure 3: New car registrations in the UK: 2013- 2019 (SMMT)

New cars registered in the UK fell by some 6 per cent in 2017 and by a further 7 per cent in 2018[19]. Vehicle registrations in 2019 were down by a further 2.4 per cent over the whole of the year according to SMMT[20]. Diesel car registrations were down 22 per cent, while petrol cars rose by 2 per cent. At the same time sales of new battery powered cars rose by 144 per cent but their share remains at only 1.6 per cent of the total market. It will take a lot more for that share to rise, including greater price incentives and many more charging points across the country. But businesses were also cautious overall with new fleet registrations rising by just 0.8 per cent in 2019 as a whole.

In parallel the BCC has been reporting the development of serious skills shortages in many sectors including the car industry where EU workers make up at least 10 per cent of the UK automotive manufacturing sector labour force. [21]

With many EU citizens deciding to leave since the referendum those still arriving from the EU to work are not sufficient to stop a serious drop in net EU migration, which was just 48,000 in the year to June 2019, the lowest since 2003. [22]

And yet the sector remains a vital part of the economy and of UK manufacturing, accounting for 12 per cent of all exports[23]. With 57 per cent of UK car production going to the EU it is no surprise that developments on the Brexit front are worrying the UK car industry, perhaps more than any other sector.

Indeed, in his letter to Nicky Morgan, former chair of the House of Commons Treasury Select Committee (and now in the Lords) on the implications of a no-deal Brexit, the then Chancellor Philip Hammond singled out the car industry for mention among the sectors most likely to be affected by a no-deal Brexit[24].

In a report of their Annual Executive Survey[25] in early January 2019, the Engineering Employers' Federation (EEF), the manufacturing association, and AIG Insurance found that Brexit was affecting manufacturing confidence negatively with the most feared issue being delays at the border[26].

What next?

As the next deadline of January 31 for exiting the EU approaches, the sector will have to brace itself for what is to come. The outcome of the forthcoming trade negotiations with the EU will be critical. Tariff-free trade would be welcome, but the issue is more one of the extra costs and disruption associated with the ending of frictionless trade with the EU, which would severely undermine the just-in-time manufacturing that has served the sector well.

More than half of car components used in car assembly in the UK are produced elsewhere and a part can move multiple times between the UK and the rest of the EU to be improved/added to before it forms part of the final assembly over here[27]. Any end to this cooperation with continental suppliers – and their cooperation in turn with the 2,500 UK suppliers – would eat away at the UK sector's competitiveness, and with it the attraction of the UK to foreign investment.

And the regional implications would be severe. Work by Dennis Novy at the University of Warwick has calculated the unintended consequences for inflation of the Brexit vote as a result of sterling's depreciation since June 2016; it concluded that the North of England, Scotland, Wales and Northern Ireland – all areas with above average import content – suffered most in terms of that inflation that followed.

The study warns that even if sterling falls no further – in fact it has recently been rising as political uncertainty at least has been lifted and the chances of another referendum have disappeared – any tariffs imposed on EU imports after Brexit would exacerbate the inflationary impact felt so far, while non-tariff barriers such as customs checks and red tape would ultimately also be damaging as they would feed into higher prices for British consumers.

This would be particularly pronounced in areas where pan-European supply chains have been well established and end up being disrupted[28]. According to SMMT calculations, a no-deal shift to the 10 per cent EU tariffs that would apply to UK cars as a third country, and 4.5 per cent tariffs on exports of components, would add some £1.8bn to the cost of exports and affect competitiveness adversely. Imports of cars from the EU would bear an extra cost of some £2.7bn, which would be hard for the sector to absorb at a time when consumers remain under pressure in their personal finances.

Looking at this analysis it is obvious that the car industry is likely to be one of the most affected by this – both in terms of costs and also consumer demand.

Multinational businesses already moving

Michael MacMahon from Oxford University[30] has looked at the impact of uncertainty over Brexit on business decisions. He concludes that "because the UK is so interconnected with other EU nations, uncertainty over Brexit has likely affected every aspect of firms' business environment". Worryingly, as he points out, a large number of companies appear to have only just realised the extent of the exposure of their business to membership of the EU – which allows them participation in global supply chains, access to labour across all skills levels, and access to all the services they need. Hence the recent rush to stockpile goods and components reported in the UK at the turn of the year.

In his piece for the 2019 Centre for Competitive Advantage in the Global Economy (Cage) report MacMahon ends up lamenting the fact that firms are in fact facing what he terms 'policy-generated uncertainty' (Brexit, one would argue, being one) as government objectives often look completely undeliverable.

But though hard-line Brexit – a no deal – was feared most because of the rules of origin, customs controls, and delays, all Brexit scenarios would make the UK production more difficult and less competitive.

Reflecting these concerns the EEF, in its briefings, has recommended that to ensure some continuity and minimise costs, if and when the UK leaves the single market, the manufacturing sector should be allowed to continue to participate in developing 'harmonised' product standards. 30

Again, on behalf of manufacturers as a whole, it also pleaded for the current health and safety landscape to be maintained after leaving the EU so as to avoid creating extra costs and disrupting business. 31

That is of course in direct contrast to how some people interpret 'taking back control', the slogan that contributed to winning the election of December 12 for the Conservatives and finally ushering in Brexit.

That interpretation says that on exiting the EU the UK is given licence to diverge its regulatory base and take advantage of that freedom to compete more aggressively with the rest of the world – and the EU.

Were that view to dominate then the chances of a deal being agreed, which allows trade to be as frictionless as possible which is what the industry would ideally want, diminishes considerably.

So uncertainty will remain. And Brexit arguments will not go away. Most economists therefore looking at the difficulties ahead expect the economy overall, to stay subdued in 2020 growing by no more than 1-1.5per cent with investment rising very slowly at best.

Cost-free Brexit for the car sector is a dream

So what is in prospect? As Mike Hawkes, chief executive of SMMT has pointed out: "Frictionless trade as part of the EU single market and customs union has driven the success of the UK automotive industry so the fact we are leaving is already painful, and already causing damage." [32] Moreover any free-trade deal with other countries, such as the one mooted with the US, would necessitate a fall in import tariffs for cars coming to the UK from the US and that could mean the loss of tens of thousands of car manufacturing and service jobs here.

A cost-free Brexit is a dream. Any added friction that augments costs to producers in what is a very tight-margin sector that has to meet tough emissions regulations and other safety standards will be affected by this[33].

The automotive sector is therefore braced for quite a rough time ahead. A longer transition period beyond December 2020 would help, but there is no guarantee that this will be on the table. What will emerge after the UK leaves remains unclear. And then there is the question of financial support. Will the sums of money that are currently earmarked for transport, including the automotive sector, under the Horizon 2020 budget agreement and the Horizon Europe that succeeds it, still flow to UK car manufacturing?

High levels of cross border research and development have been important in assisting competitiveness in the sector. In early January 2020 it was suggested that the new government's appetite to spend more supporting industry, R&D and the regions on the back of relaxed fiscal rules, while borrowing costs remained at their current near record low levels, might provide some relief.

But for the sector in the end much will depend on what type of trade agreement we strike with the EU. Will we get there? And what is more, will we get there in a year which seems to be the new deadline when the transition period is due to come to an end? Don't hold your breath.

Notes

1. https://www.smmt.co.uk/industry-topics/uk-automotive/
2. https://www.bbc.co.uk/news/business-47055188
3. https://www.ons.gov.uk/economy/grossdomesticproductgdp/bulletins/businessinvestment/julytoseptember2019revisedresults
4. https://tradingeconomics.com/united-kingdom/business-confidence

5. https://www.bbc.co.uk/news/business-47055188
6. https://www.smmt.co.uk/2018/11/no-deal-brexit-catastrophic-blow-to-british-auto-industry-warn-businesses-in-new-survey/
7. https://www.quora.com/Are-there-any-remaining-British-owned-car-manufacturing-companies
8. https://www.theguardian.com/business/2019/feb/02/nissan-x-trail-uk-brexit
9. https://www.bbc.co.uk/news/business-47287386
10. https://www.theguardian.com/business/2019/feb/18/hondas-exit-is-based-on-many-factors-but-brexit-is-certainly-one
11. https://www.theguardian.com/business/2019/feb/18/workers-blame-brexit-for-demise-of-hondas-swindon-plant
12. https://news.sky.com/story/honda-to-stop-production-for-six-days-after-brexit-11603875
13. https://www.theguardian.com/business/2019/may/20/jaguar-land-rover-record-loss-chinese-market-diesel-sales
14. https://www.bbc.co.uk/news/business-46822706
15. https://news.sky.com/story/honda-to-stop-production-for-six-days-after-brexit-11603875
16. https://www.theguardian.com/business/2019/dec/20/car-plant-shutdowns-around-brexit-deadline-hit-uk-production
17. https://www.theguardian.com/business/2019/aug/29/british-car-industry-suffers-worst-period-of-decline-since-2001
18. https://www.driving.co.uk/news/business/british-car-makers-claim-brexit-fears-forcing-investment-away-industry/
19. https://www.autocar.co.uk/car-news/industry/uk-car-registrations-fall-68-2018-plus-2018s-best-sellers-revealed
20. https://www.smmt.co.uk/vehicle-data/car-registrations/
21. https://www.smmt.co.uk/industry-topics/brexit/brexit-issue-papers/
22. https://www.bbc.co.uk/news/uk-50586338
23. Autocar12 August 2018
24. https://assets.publishing.service.gov.uk/government/uploads/system/uploads/attachment_data/file/735881/180823_CX_to_Chair_of_TSC_Nicky_Morgan_.pdf
25. https://www.insider.co.uk/news/brexit-manufacturers-eef-aig-survey-13821842
26. https://uk.reuters.com/article/uk-britain-eu-manufacturers/uk-factories-view-border-delays-as-a-major-brexit-risk-eef-idUKKCN1P1006
27. https://www.theguardian.com/business/2017/mar/03/brexit-uk-car-industry-mini-britain-eu
28. Did the Brexit vote lead to higher UK inflation? Dennis Novy, University of Warwick and Centre for Competitive Advantage in the Global Economy (CAGE) policy report, Social Market Foundation, 2019
29. The macroeconomics of uncertainty; Michael McMahon, University of Oxford and CAGE, Social Market Foundation, 2019

30. https://www.eef.org.uk/campaigning/campaigns-and-issues/current-campaigns/manufacturing-and-europe
31. https://www.eef.org.uk/about-eef/media-news-and-insights/media-releases/2018/oct/nw-manufacturers-call-for-uk-to-stay-in-european-health-safety-regime-post-brexit-eefarco-survey
32. https://www.smmt.co.uk/2018/11/no-deal-brexit-catastrophic-blow-to-british-auto-industry-warn-businesses-in-new-survey/
33. https://www.smmt.co.uk/2018/11/no-deal-brexit-catastrophic-blow-to-british-auto-industry-warn-businesses-in-new-survey/

About the contributor

Vicky Pryce is a visiting professor at Birmingham City University, a former joint head of the UK Government Economic Service (GES), a member of the Economic Advisory Group at the British Chambers of Commerce (BCC) and on the board of the Centre for Economics and Business Research (CEBR).

Chapter 5

Manufacturing heading out, distribution moving in – the effects of Brexit

Hamid Moradlou, Hendrik Reefke and Heather Skipworth explain the reasons why Brexit may mean an increasing level of manufacturing may be offshored to Europe, while distribution centres head in turn to the UK

How has the prospect of the UK leaving the European Union affected the location decisions of UK manufacturers and distributors with customers in the EU? How has Brexit influenced supply-chain decisions regarding supplier location? And which individual factors – or drivers – feature most prominently in influencing these decisions?

A survey study conducted at the School of Management, Cranfield University, provides answers to these questions.

Surveying a panel comprising experts selected from various economically-important industries (such as automotive, aerospace, and FMCG), as well as consultancies, governmental organisations, and academia, respondents were taken through four iterative rounds of data collection, also called Delphi research approach (Reefke & Sundaram, 2017, 2018), between December 2018 and November 2019, with each round influencing the research outcomes and direction of the following rounds.

Uncertainty shaping decisions

The first finding was that despite government protestations to the contrary, industry was far from sanguine about the impact of Brexit – Brexit (and Brexit uncertainty) was indeed shaping corporate thought processes.

Followings are number of viewpoints reproduced in Figure 1 below:

> "For price-sensitive products, companies are actively investigating alternative suppliers, due to concerns over such things as tariffs and Country of Origin rules."
>
> "Decisions on where to (re)locate manufacturing facilities are currently being delayed, and investment decisions are being postponed."
>
> "Companies are relocating manufacturing, but are not always directly attributing the reason solely to Brexit. Brexit has played at least some part in the decision to cease manufacturing in the UK, but there are additional factors."
>
> "Actually, in the short and/or medium term — within a year, say — securing and switching to alternative suppliers is not really an option." [NB: Quotation edited for clarity and grammatical accuracy.]

Figure 1: Representative respondent viewpoints

In deciding whether to relocate or add manufacturing facilities or distribution centres in response to Brexit, it is clear that manufacturers and distributors face subtly different challenges. Distributors, for example, are expected to face a lower overall capital cost of adding or moving a location, as well as a lower level of complexity—particularly if they choose to use the services of a third-party service provider. Whereas manufacturers also have the option of contract manufacturing, the costs and complexities of this are much higher.

Figures 2a and 2b respectively present the likely impact of Brexit on manufacturers' and distributors' location decisions. As the results indicate, it is likely that Brexit will lead to more manufacturing companies shifting their facilities to the EU, in other words offshore their manufacturing activities (Moradlou & Backhouse 2016), while for distributors it appears that Brexit will result in more distribution centres coming to the UK. This can be seen as reshoring strategy (Moradlou, et al. 2017).

WHAT IS THE LIKELY IMPACT OF BREXIT ON MANUFACTURING LOCATION...

Bringing manufacturing facilities... 0.00% 0.00% 88.00%
Bringing Suppliers to the UK 12.00%

0.00% 20.00% 40.00% 60.00% 80.00% 100.00%

Figure 2a: Impact of Brexit on manufacturing location decisions

WHAT IS THE LIKELY IMPACT OF BREXIT ON LOCATION DECISION WITH RESPECT TO DISTRIBUTION CENTRES?

12.00% 80.00%
Bringing 3rd party distribution... 4.00% 4.00%

0.00% 20.00% 40.00% 60.00% 80.00%

Figure 1b: Impact of Brexit on distribution centre location decisions

Which factors ('drivers') are taken into consideration, and how do they rank against each other? Undoubtedly, moving—or adding—a manufacturing location is not a decision to be taken lightly.

In order to arrive at such decision number of factors will play important role (Tate & Bals 2017). Here are the results from the Delphi study: Table 1 ranks the drivers behind the shift in manufacturing production from the UK to EU, based on their relative importance. The top five drivers motivating companies to move out of the UK are access to the EU market; potential delays in product delivery due to new border controls; higher costs through

	Drivers for moving manufacturing to the EU
1	Access to the EU market
2	Delays in product delivery due to new border control
3	Higher costs through new tariffs of import/export to the EU
4	Access to international markets through EU trade deals
5	Proximity to customers in the EU
6	Higher non-tariff costs, such as inventory levels, of import/export to the EU
7	EU approval procedures (e.g. for medicines/drugs) and respective access to market
8	Uncertainty and fear
9	Uncertain regulations with respect to customs arrangements
10	Access to suppliers
11	Market competition forces/encourages a move to the EU
12	Favourable currency conditions (exchange rates, stability, same currency trades, etc.)
13	EU standard regulations
14	Higher stability (political, financial, regulations, etc.) of the destination country
15	Business consolidation to other facilities
16	Declining demand and unprofitable plants in the UK
17	Government incentives offered by EU countries
18	Access to skilled labour
19	Access to research and development
20	Lower cost of manufacturing in the EU

Table 1: Drivers for moving manufacturing to the EU

new tariffs of import/export to the EU; access to international markets through EU trade deals; and proximity to customers in the EU.

On the other hand, the least important five factors influencing the relocation of manufacturing facilities to the EU are lower cost of manufacturing in the EU; access to research and development; access to skilled labour; government incentives offered by EU countries; and declining demand and unprofitable plants in the UK.The top five drivers for keeping the production in the UK are proximity to customers in the UK; the avoidance of non-tariff costs (such as border delays and inventory levels) of importing to the UK; the high cost of transferring operations; the avoidance of tariff costs when importing to the UK; and access to R&D.

	Drivers for keeping manufacturing in the UK
1	Proximity to customers in the UK
2	To avoid non-tariff costs (such as border delays and inventory levels) of importing to the UK
3	High cost of transferring operations
4	To avoid tariff costs of importing to the UK
5	Access to research and development
6	Customer service agreements
7	Access to suppliers
8	Uncertain regulations (customs arrangements)
9	Government incentives offered by the UK
10	Possible removal or lowering of taxation
11	UK Research & Development taxation regulations
12	Access to labour
13	Lower cost of manufacturing in the UK

Table 2: Drivers for keeping manufacturing in the UK

Conversely, the least important five drivers for retaining manufacturing in the UK are seen as a lower cost of manufacturing in the UK; access to labour; access to UK R&D taxation incentives; and the possible removal or lowering of other taxation and location incentives offered by the UK government.

Considering the bottom drivers for both leaving the UK and staying in the UK, it is evident that the least important drivers for moving facilities in this scenario are around the cost of labour and cost of production, indicating that these type of costs are not driving manufacturing facility location decisions.

Hence companies are actively looking for ways to create customer value as well as increase their profit rather than merely considering the cost savings aspects (Ellram et al. 2013). This is also in contradiction to what is traditionally known to be the main reasons behind offshoring decisions (Moradlou & Tate, 2018). On the other hand, market access and uncertainties regarding tariff barriers are seen as very important in the location decision.

Finally, Table 3 presents the most impacted industry sectors, as perceived by respondents. Notably, the pharmaceutical, automotive, healthcare and food industries are consistently seen as industries in which every part of the supply chain—manufacturing, distribution, and the supplier base—is likely to be impacted by Brexit. These findings are in line with studies done by Hendry et al. (2019) focusing on food supply chain and Bailey and De Propris (2017) focusing on automotive sector.

Conclusion

It is clear that Brexit, in the interval between the 2016 referendum result and our final Delphi survey in November 2019, has shaped corporate decision-making processes regarding the location of supply chain activities. For the first time in more than 40 years, manufacturers and distributors have had to contemplate tariff barriers, non-tariff barriers, and the fundamentals of market access in their UK-EU trade deliberations.

	Manufact'g	Suppliers	Distribution
1	Pharmaceut'l	Pharmaceut'l	Pharmaceut'l
2	Automotive	Automotive	Healthcare
3	Healthcare	Food	Automotive
4	Food	Healthcare	Food
5	Aerospace	Aerospace	Aerospace
6	FMCG	Electronic	FMCG
7	Electronic	FMCG	Electronic
8	Fashion	Fashion	Fashion

Table 3: Industries mostly impacted by Brexit

One consequence, as these survey findings make clear, is that some manufacturing activity is likely to move offshore, away from the UK and to the EU. Equally clearly, companies serving the UK directly from the EU are likely to invest in UK-based distribution centres and inventory holdings. In both cases, the overall consequence is likely to be some erosion of manufacturing economies of scale, due to increased production fragmentation, and lower levels of inventory turn.

Finally, in contrast to economic theory, the relative cost of labour and the relative cost of production appeared to have little influence on the EU-UK location decision. Instead it is issues such as market access, trade frictions, and potential tariffs that are seen as more important. Whatever the exact nature of EU-UK trade relations going forward, post-Brexit, the implications for policymakers are clear.

References

Bailey, D. and De Propris, L. (2017) 'Brexit and the UK Automotive Industry', National Institute Economic Review, 242(1), pp. R51–R59. doi: 10.1177/002795011724200114.

Ellram, L. M., Tate, W. L. and Petersen, K. J. (2013) 'Offshoring And Reshoring : An Update On The Manufacturing Location Decision', Journal of Supply Chain Management, 49(2), pp. 14–22.

Hendry, L. C., Stevenson, M., MacBryde, J., Ball, P., Sayed, M., & Liu, L. (2019). Local food supply chain resilience to constitutional change: The Brexit effect. International Journal of Operations & Production Management, 39(3), 429-453.

Moradlou, H. and Backhouse, C. J. (2016) 'A review of manufacturing re-shoring in the context of customer-focused postponement strategies', Proceedings of the Institution of Mechanical Engineers, Part B: Journal of Engineering Manufacture, 230(9), pp. 1561–1571. doi: 10.1177/0954405415623486.

Moradlou, H., Backhouse, C. and Ranganathan, R. (2017) 'Responsiveness, the primary reason behind re-shoring manufacturing activities to the UK: An Indian industry perspective', International Journal of Physical Distribution and Logistics Management, 47(2–3), pp. 222–236. doi: 10.1108/IJPDLM-06-2015-0149.

Moradlou, H. and Tate, W. (2018) 'Reshoring and additive manufacturing', World Review of Intermodal Transportation Research, 7(3), pp. 241–263. doi: 10.1504/WRITR.2018.093564.

Reefke, H. and Sundaram, D. (2017) 'Key themes and research opportunities in sustainable supply chain management – identification and evaluation', Omega (United Kingdom). Elsevier, 66, pp. 195–211. doi: 10.1016/j.omega.2016.02.003

Reefke, H. and Sundaram, D. (2018) 'Sustainable supply chain management: Decision models for transformation and maturity', Decision Support Systems. Elsevier, 113(July), pp. 56–72. doi: 10.1016/j.dss.2018.07.002.

Tate, W. L. and Bals, L. (2017) 'Outsourcing/offshoring insights: going beyond reshoring to rightshoring', International Journal of Physical Distribution and Logistics Management, 47(2–3), pp. 106–113. doi: 10.1108/IJPDLM-11-2016-0314.

About the contributors

Dr Hamid Moradlou is a lecturer in supply chain management at Cranfield University, School of Management. His research interests mainly focuses on investigating the offshoring and re-shoring phenomenon in developed countries and the impacts of new generation of technologies, industry 4.0, on manufacturing location decision.

Dr Hendrik Reefke is a lecturer in supply chain management at Cranfield University, School of Management. He is an active researcher, focusing primarily on sustainable supply chain management, service supply chains, warehousing, as well as performance measurement and reporting.

Dr Heather Skipworth is an associate professor in supply chain management at Cranfield University, School of Management. Her particular areas of research interest include: agile and responsive supply chains; segmented supply chain strategy and alignment; outsourcing of logistics and procurement in the NHS; and supply chain risk.

Chapter 6

A compelling event requiring real change

In the television show, *Deal or No Deal*, the uncertainty is built until the very last box is opened. With Brexit, it seems they've managed to increase the suspense as someone keeps moving the box! We have shifted from one level of uncertainty to the next. Latest results continue to seriously affect the automotive industry. Tom Leeson, automotive industry specialist at OpenText, asks: Is it possible to prepare for Brexit?

Despite recent progress Brexit remains at a point where we can't really be certain about the things we're certain about. In April 2019 UK car manufacturing stood down more than 6000 staff[1] and almost halved national car production[2]. That had been contingency planning for a no-deal Brexit. So, no deal is off the table? Well, no. In fact, in some macabre way it has become a potential bargaining chip. Meanwhile this is a political crisis that continues to affect every part of business.

The Markit/CIPS UK manufacturing purchasing managers' index[3] (PMI) continues to fall and the result for November 2019 at 45.6 (down from 49.1), is significant in being the lowest since July 2012. Readings below 50 per cent denote contraction. The economic slowdown has led Tom Crotty[4], chairman of the CBI's manufacturing council, to comment: "Every day that goes by without a resolution results in more businesses putting off investment and stockpiling goods in order to soften the blow from a potentially disastrous no-deal Brexit."

Nowhere is this slowdown more apparent than the automotive industry. The Society of Motor Manufacturers and Traders[5] (SMMT) reported that 2019 saw a third year of decline in UK cars registrations, down a further 2 per cent year on year. Mike Hawes, chief executive of SMMT attributes weak consumer confidence to Brexit and diesel uncertainty. And the two are not unrelated. Hawes said: "A stalling market will hinder industry's ability to meet stringent new CO2 targets" [6].

The SMMT[7] had previously reported that production fell 9.1 per cent in 2018 to 1.52m vehicles, with output for UK market and exports falling 16.3 per cent and 7.3 per cent respectively. The industry body suggests that investment in the sector has almost halved in 12 months.

Hawes[8] said that the worst effect of Brexit will be caused by "the permanent devastation caused by severing our frictionless trade links overnight, not just with the EU but with the many other global markets with which we currently trade freely".

The scale of Brexit in UK auto

In a single day in the UK Automotive sector sees:

- 1100 trucks from the EU delivering £35m components, 'just in time' from the European Union.
- 6400 cars and 10500 engines manufactured in UK facilities with 54 per cent engines and 80 per cent of cars exported worldwide. Nearly 3000 of those cars go back to the EU.

Furthermore:

- With global skill shortages in the manufacturing industry at least one in ten people employed in the UK automotive manufacturing sector are from elsewhere in the EU.
- Currently more than 800,000 people are dependent on the sector[9]
- The motor industry contributed £20.2bn to the UK economy (2018) [10]

Meanwhile, the original B-Day (March 29, 2019), B-Day plus one (April 12, 2019), and B-Day plus two (October 31, 2019) have all come and gone.

In that time an 'awful' lot has happened, but has anything really changed? Political turmoil has been at crisis level and Brexit has fundamentally changed the face of UK politics.

It continues to be difficult to predict the future outcome but with the recent general election changing the political landscape inside Westminster, B-Day January 31 is looking more certain.

And so it will be on to the next stage of trade deal negotiations with the EU; the uncertainty continuing until December 2020, which is an ambitious timeframe in which to negotiate a trade deal with EU. With this date comes yet another hard-stop for the UK government it would appear, and a potential no deal remains.

Automakers have warned that if the British exit from the EU results in tariffs, UK-built vehicles will become uncompetitive for sale to mainland Europe[11]. And Jaguar Land Rover(JLR) CEO Dr Ralf Speth has said the 'wrong' Brexit would cost the UK car industry tens of thousands of jobs.

While remaining optimistic towards Sunderland's continuous development as an international automotive hub, Nissan Europe chairman Gianluca de Ficchy told *Automotive News Europe* that a hard Brexit resulting in World Trade Origination (WTO) tariffs would make business unsustainable at Sunderland where 70 per cent of vehicle production in exported to Europe. Meanwhile Toyota built just over 8 per cent of Britain's total car production last year. A less than favourable deal could end its manufacturing in the UK.

As Brexit enters its final phase, automotive is likely to be prioritised in the negotiations particularly for Germany, Poland, Austria, Romania and the Czech Republic, which have all singled out the importance of cars and auto parts. The UK imported 1.5m autos from the EU in 2018, worth €35bn according to Bloomberg Intelligence[12].

Since my initial engagement on this Brexit journey I was quick to advocate 'Plan for the worst and hope for the best' as a preparation approach. And while I appreciate for many this recommendation would involve costs to mitigate for some things that might not come to fruition, delaying in trying to plan in some way will undoubtably lead to greater costs and impacts in the long run.

Even if a no deal scenario is avoided, it is almost impossible to conceive that trade between the UK and the EU will be as friction free as it is now. This was the focus of a report *Brexit and the UK Automotive Industry*[13] conducted by OpenText and the Centre of Brexit Studies. We looked at the UK's automotive industry and how it was preparing for Brexit.

Our research study set out to identify the likely implications that different Brexit options could have on the industry in five key business areas: supply chain management; operations and logistics; human resource management; regulations and compliance; and customer communications.

Key recommendations

The report set out a number of key recommendations about how, deal or no deal, automotive companies could prepare for Brexit:

- Automotive companies need to have good enterprise information management (EIM) [14] policies in place for managing and reporting on contracts to implement changes and mitigate risks. Managing information such as contracts digitally helps establish governance processes that will help amend existing contracts and generate new contracts as the details of Brexit become law.
- Original equipment manufacturers (OEMs) and suppliers need to have a strong information governance [15] strategy in place to ensure compliance with any new regulatory requirements or checks. Getting control over the acquisition, management, retention and disposal of all the information within a business means, no matter what the impact of Brexit, businesses will be better prepared. A good use case here (namely for larger companies) would be to use information management to assist in attaining the status of authorised economic operator (AEO).
- More emphasis on workforce planning and skills development is needed in the likelihood that Brexit further restricts the supply of immigrant labour. Human resource managers will most likely face a different talent market post Brexit and should consider transforming employee information, such that it is easily accessible, particularly relating to employee skills and training needs that support them through any transition needs. Recruitment teams would benefit from a digital support environment aligned to the needs of the business in recruiting missing skills.
- Closer communication and collaboration between automotive manufacturers, partners and customers is needed to ensure a free flow of information. Digital technology can be implemented such that information exchange is transacted and communicated in an efficient and consistent manner. It is essential that the OEMs can react quickly to supply chain changes and communicate those

changes in a way that's personalised to the business needs of each partner.

- Automotive manufacturers need to have an improved understanding of their supply chain, particularly with respect to any new documentation and compliance requirements that might be put in place. Companies should consider adopting a managed services approach to assist the onboarding and transactions management of both existing and new suppliers because of any changes. This approach moves towards digitizing the supply chain while at the same time freeing up internal resources to focus on other priorities.
- Companies should review their current processes for the delivery of good and customs procedures and adapt where applicable. In particular, they should look to achieving as frictionless trade as possible by providing good connection to customs requirements and the use of pre-clearance and digital documentation such as advanced shipping notices (ASN) to support risk-assessment of goods prior to entry.

In my opinion, improved EIM lies at the heart of any technology-driven approach to meeting whatever Brexit environment the automotive industry finds itself in. For example, while a completely technological solution to cross-border trade is still some way off, EIM uses platforms that exist today to ease the process of supply chain management and customs clearance.

This technology can help replace physical infrastructure to enable organisations to meet the new customs arrangements, but this will revolve around the quick, effective and intelligent sharing of information. For example, advanced shipping notices (ASNs) could form a basis to facilitate pre-arrival clearance, so reducing potential bottlenecks at the borders.

Data transforming businesses

In this fourth industrial revolution, where the driving asset for business success is data, all industries, including manufacturing, are transforming the ways they will do business in the future.

The automotive industry has been at the forefront of technology adoption since the 1980s when people like me were headhunted into the industry from the aerospace sector. This has been transformational for automakers ever since. Technology has been a necessity to enable developments and innovations in the modern motor vehicle.

Like all manufacturing industries, the automotive sector face a gauntlet of challenges and success is largely contingent upon being able to adapt and overcome.

With the industry entering into a time of significant change and disruption, automakers will need to deploy digital transformation solutions to increase the efficiency of their business and to be competitive. The same solutions could help address many of the challenges posed by Brexit by streamlining and automating business processes, so making a business more agile and robust through better information utilisation that saves time and money.

The automotive industry has been using digital technology to innovate the industry for many years. Often justification in such investment requires a compelling event to trigger change. As one of the biggest events in economic history – for the UK, EU and beyond – Brexit is such a compelling event.

Notes

1. https://www.theguardian.com/politics/2019/apr/11/uk-stands-down-6000-no-deal-brexit-staff-after-spending-15bn
2. https://www.bbc.co.uk/news/business-48451024
3. https://www.manufacturingglobal.com/technology/uk-car-sales-hit-six-year-low-brexit-and-emissions-uncertainty
4. https://www.cbi.org.uk/media-centre/articles/brexit-uncertainty-sees-stockpiling-race-to-post-financial-crisis-peak-cbi/
5. https://www.manufacturingglobal.com/technology/uk-car-sales-hit-six-year-low-brexit-and-emissions-uncertainty
6. https://www.smmt.co.uk/2020/01/record-year-for-zero-emission-cars-fails-to-reboot-uk-market-as-sector-calls-for-supportive-policies-to-boost-uptake/
7. https://www.bbc.co.uk/news/business-47055188
8. Ibid
9. https://www.statista.com/topics/1982/the-uk-automotive-industry/
10. Ibid
11. https://europe.autonews.com/automakers/johnsons-uk-election-win-clears-path-brexit

12. https://europe.autonews.com/automakers/auto-industry-center-future-brexit-battles
13. https://bcuassets.blob.core.windows.net/docs/report-for-opentext--deliverable-b-final-131880562823173347.pdf
14. https://blogs.opentext.com/enterprise-information-management-eim/
15. https://www.bcu.ac.uk/centre-for-brexit-studies/reports

About the contributor

Tom Leeson is Senior Industry Strategist for the manufacturing sector at OpenText. He is an engineer by trade and a mathematician by education. He has nearly 40 years of experience working in the manufacturing sector. First within aerospace, automotive and discrete manufacturing companies introducing computational techniques before moving into the engineering and manufacturing IT sector. Over the last 22 years Tom has fulfilled various senior roles with manufacturing software specialists Dassault Systemes, SmarTeam PLM, Computervision, PTC and the Artificial Intelligence Company Aion Corp.

Chapter 7

What a difference a decisive election makes

The British auto industry may be freed from Brexit indecision, says Neil Winton, but it can't escape its many existential problems

Chaos, indecision and weakness of the last three years have been replaced by a government with a powerful majority in parliament, and a clear vision of what it wants for British business in general and the auto industry in particular – namely a free-trade arrangement with the European Union (EU).

A year ago, the outlook for the British auto industry looked bleak and uncertain as Brexit talks stumbled. Investment was on hold because the future of Britain's trade with the EU was impossible to predict. Sales of cars and SUVs slipped, as worries about the future restrained private buyers.

The then government's Brexit negotiating position with the EU looked weak with expectations that a free-trade deal would be denied. A World Trade Organisation tariff regime loomed.

Britain had a government unable to act effectively because it lacked a parliamentary majority, and no realistic prospect of acquiring one. Britain's 'Remainer' political faction seemed to have the upper hand. It had the power in parliament to stop the progress of Brexit, but not enough to kill it off. It convinced EU negotiators that Brexit might well be reversed if they could just hold their nerve.

The prospects of a deal which wasn't far short of Britain actually remaining a member of the EU, without the voting rights, loomed large. That would have been a dream outcome for the EU; all the advantages of free trade with a huge market, without Britain's semi-detached trouble-making that it could wield as an EU member.

Bleating in unison

The British auto industry representatives were bleating in unison, so desperate were they to avoid any change in their cosy arrangements with the EU. But it turned out that for those willing to peak behind the scenes, this status quo, which the likes of the Society of Motor Manufacturers and Traders (SMMT) wanted to hang on to so desperately, hadn't been providing the benefits spelled out on the tin.

Data from the Office of National Statistics (ONS) showed Britain's auto trade with the EU over the last 20 years had barely gained in volume, while imports soared. At the same time exports with the rest of the world under WTO rules had advanced hugely, despite the tariffs.

And again counter-intuitively, many countries, the US for example, had a more successful record of general trading into the EU over a 20-year period with a 10 per cent tariff, than Britain had from inside the free-trade zone.

During the dark, indecisive days of Brexit negotiations, one problem loomed large for the industry. Would big manufacturers like Nissan, Toyota and Honda (now about to upsticks and leave anyway) get a deal that would allow them not only to trade freely with the EU, but guarantee smooth running of its complicated supply lines from across Europe?

Now that seems close to becoming reality, the point has become moot. Ironically, early last year Japan and the EU finally signed a free-trade agreement which might well make their British factories redundant in the long term.

The election result of December 12 changes everything. Britain formally left the EU on January 31, 2020, and there is an 11-month period to negotiate the free-trade deal, with a couple of hurdles along the way. The EU now knows that Britain is definitely leaving, so its negotiators can forget the politics and pursue a deal which benefits both sides.

And despite the frenzied politicking and blind panic of the SMMT, it is clear the auto industry need not fear having to trade with the world under WTO rules. So sunlit uplands await the British auto industry?

Decade of disruption

Maybe, but the global industry faces a decade of disruption as electric cars and computer- driven ones gradually replace conventional vehicles. The whole idea of individual car ownership is being questioned. And it's not clear who the winners may be – perhaps cash-rich high-tech interlopers – or where they will be located.

Peter Wells, Professor of Business and Sustainability at Cardiff Business School, said Britain's mass-market auto industry has been weakening for some time: "The future of the UK automotive industry is particularly bleak because the decision to leave the EU, with all the economic uncertainty and probable added cost entailed, comes at a time of massive and rapid technological and business convulsions sweeping through the industry," he said.

Wells said even before the exit decision it was clear the UK was becoming too expensive to compete in the lower margin segments, despite good quality and productivity.

Britain's auto industry may return to pre-EU conditions where, as imports become more expensive and exports more difficult, UK output may focus on the home market. This might work if cars become more of a commodity and less of a status symbol.

Wells said the long-term future for the industry is more likely to be a smaller domestic industry producing high-margin vehicles.

Other experts say there will be big challenges for the auto industry outside of the EU, but it should thrive nonetheless. Any free-trade deal with the EU will be relatively easy because it really amounts to simply consolidating what already exists.

The industry will have to raise productivity because it will no longer be able to hide behind the 10 per cent tariff barrier provided by the EU. The industry won't welcome having to improve efficiency but the likes of Jaguar Land Rover (JLR) already manage to do this very successfully. Now they will be able to source components not just from the EU but also the rest of the world.

Japanese quandary

The free-trade deal with Japan raises the question about whether Toyota and Nissan would want to remain in the UK even if it were firmly in the EU for the long term. It's unlikely in the short term that these companies would want to shut down very efficient factories because big global manufacturers need to insure themselves against things like exchange rate fluctuations and perhaps tariff wars too. Having a paid-for alternative makes good business sense.

Phil Radford, trade analyst and author of nothingtofear.co.uk, said if a free trade deal is agreed, exports to the EU will be stagnant, as they have over the last 20 years. Japanese manufacturers will eventually withdraw because there won't be a competitive advantage from staying. Premium manufacturers like JLR and BMW's Mini will continue to invest in mainland Europe production, and of course when they export to say, the US, those sales won't count as UK exports.

"Thus the impact of an FTA will not just be the mid-term end to UK-based mass-market motor market manufacturing, but a steady diminution of UK premium marque motor manufacturing," Radford said.

Nobody, at least in the short-term, now seems to expect no deal, but if there was a failure, Radford initially expects the British government to mirror the EU 10 per cent tariff. This would save the mass market industry in the short term, but the likes of Nissan and Toyota would have to radically sharpen their business model, or leave.

"The key thing with the Japanese manufacturers is that they have signally failed to create the sort of vast market in the EU that would justify the UK needing an FTA that covered autos post-Brexit," Radford said.

From 2000 to 2018, Nissan raised its market share in Europe from 2.9 to 3.2 per cent, Toyota from 3.6 to 4.5 per cent, and Honda's fell from 1.3 to 0.9 per cent, according to carsalesbase.com. In contrast in the US, Nissan's market share rose from 3.9 to 7.8 per cent, Toyota advanced from 8 to 12.3 per cent, while Honda spurted from 5.9 to 8.3 per cent

Long-term industry direction

Fitch Solutions Macro Research welcomed the fact a clear path was being mapped to finally leave the EU. It pointed out that the long impasse over the Brexit issue had led to many manufacturers postponing or cancelling investment, and that this wouldn't be reignited until the long-term direction of the industry in Britain had been re-established.

"There are carmakers waiting for concrete details on future trade to make decisions over their UK operations, such as PSA Groupe, which has said the future of its Vauxhall plant in the UK depends on favourable Brexit conditions. With this in mind, any delays to a long-term trade deal would pose considerable risk to the production side of the industry," Fitch said in a report.

Automotive consultancy ICDP welcomed what it called the first clarity about Brexit in more than three years, as the UK will now definitely be leaving the EU, but it also opened up a new phase of uncertainty as the negotiations between Britain and the EU were likely to be complicated. ICDP said in a report, published before the British government said it would legislate to stop an extension of the talks, that there probably would be extensions to the transition period.

This is likely to be true because even if the British government says there will no extension, the EU might not go along with that. And if a short extension of hours or days was required, it seems unlikely the UK would call the whole thing off.

ICDP also expected a delay before any serious manufacturing investment was resumed: "Manufacturers considering their investments in the UK will have no choice but to play safe and put their money elsewhere, and the uncertainty will feed in to the general economy, so that the car market itself will be held back at a time when it needs confidence to invest," ICDP said.

Unanswered questions

Consultancy Capgemini was loathe to speculate on how the saga would end: "There are so many unanswered questions. Will Brexit have a major impact on the economy? How will consumers react; will there be a drawback in consumer spend? It's not possible to comment at this stage, there are so many factors that could play in this new situation that it would be pure speculation," said Capgemini Global Automotive Lead, Markus Winkler.

Currently, Britain hosts big car factories from Toyota and Nissan, while Honda has announced it was pulling out in 2021. There is JLR and BMW's Mini and Rolls Royce. Vauxhall, now a part of PSA Groupe, operates a big plant at Ellesmere Port, near Liverpool. There are also specialist vehicle makers like VW's Bentley, McLaren, and Lotus.

HS2 solution

Trying to predict the long-term future of the auto industry is indeed more difficult than ever. Imagine there's an early, say 2025, breakthrough in computerised cars. If you could click on an app on your phone, and wherever you were in the country, (well not Dartmoor or the Scottish Highlands) an anonymous little high-tech bubble appeared within two minutes. You'd never need to buy your own car again, and would you really care if was a Skoda or a BMW?

And this would solve another problem. When HS2 is finally built, probably for £200bn, nobody will want to travel by train anymore anyway, but it will make a magnificent high-speed track for autonomous cars going north and south.

About the contributor
Neil Winton is a *Forbes* contributor, writing about the global automotive industry. He worked for Reuters for more than 30 years with beat assignments including Science and Technology, European Automotive, and Millennium Bug. He also wrote the European Perspective column for the *Detroit News*, and publishes the automotive analysis website www.WintonsWorld.com. Contact him at neil.winton@btinternet.com or twitter @wintonsauto

Chapter 8

The form of Brexit will still be critical for UK auto

David Bailey explains that it is not just leaving the EU that is important, but that the manner of leaving will really count

The period since the 2016 referendum has been a turbulent one for UK manufacturing in general and UK auto in particular.

By 2018-2019 something of a 'perfect storm' had hit the auto industry. The industry faced a triple whammy of declining sales in China (as the world's largest car market contracted after 20 years of breakneck growth), a massive shift away from diesels across Europe in the wake of the VW Dieselgate scandal, and Brexit uncertainty slowing the UK market and investment.

It was in this difficult environment that over 2018-19 Jaguar Land Rover (JLR) announced nearly 6,000 job cuts. Other bad news in this period included confirmation that Honda was shutting its Swindon plant and Ford its Bridgend plant, while Nissan reversed its decision to build the X-Trail model at Sunderland from 2020, citing Brexit as a complicating factor, and scrapped further *Infiniti* brand production at the plant.

Both auto sales and output continued to fall through 2019, with car registrations down by 2.4 per cent[1] and output by 14.5 per cent through to November.[2] More broadly, while manufacturing underwent something of a stockpiling boost ahead of the original March Brexit deadline, output then stagnated. By the year end UK manufacturing was contracting at its fastest rate in seven years as new orders fell and Brexit buffer stocks were run down, in turn acting as a drag on economic growth.[3]

A few investments, by the likes of JLR in electric vehicle production[4] and Aston Martin in its new DBX model[5] stood out as positive stories, but investment in the auto sector in particular stalled amidst Brexit uncertainty over the nature of the future trading relationship with the EU, falling by some 80 per cent over the last three years.[6]

The impact on production

That uncertainty also had an impact on output. Auto assemblers including JLR, Toyota and BMW shut down assembly operations in both April and October to avoid disruption around the time of the UK's scheduled departure dates from the EU.

JLR's chief executive Ralf Speth said the firm had no choice but to stop production lines at its four UK plants (Solihull, Castle Bromwich, Wolverhampton and Halewood), stating that the firm needed 20 million parts a day; every part had to be available when needed and just in time.

The latter point illustrates the vulnerability of manufacturing (and not just auto) that relies on just-in-time' (JIT) supply chains to any form of Brexit that could create delays and supply-chain disruption.

Essentially, disruption arising under either a no-deal Brexit at the end of 2020 or even a bare bones Canada-style free-trade-agreement could throw a major spanner in the works of JIT systems commonly used across UK and EU manufacturing.

No deal at the end of 2020 would be especially damaging as tariffs of 10 per cent would apply on exported cars. A no-deal Brexit on WTO terms could add around £3bn a year to UK's auto's costs through tariffs alone, as Ian Henry illustrates in this volume (see chapter 3), with additional non-tariff barrier costs (such as form filling, customs delays and stockpiling costs) coming on top.

Analysts like Henry have forecast a short-term production hit from no deal of at least 175,000 cars a year (that's not including the Honda closure), which is more than 10 per cent of UK car output.[7] Longer term, with no deal there is a significant risk that firms will consider shifting production activities outside of the UK such that the loss of output could be much higher (see Cox and Oakley in chapter 1 in this volume).

In such a scenario there could be considerable job losses in the Midlands and North – including constituencies recently won by the Conservatives when Labour's 'Red Wall' crumbled. To what extent newly elected Conservative MPs in such areas listen to the views of manufacturing and auto makers could be an interesting dynamic in the government.

The actual deal could be damaging

While no deal is seen by many in industry as highly damaging[8], even a limited trade deal that simply eliminates most tariffs – of the sort envisaged in the latest political declaration – could still cause severe headaches for industry given issues of regulatory divergence and through the UK being outside the EU customs union.

That means another year of uncertainty for big auto assemblers, which in turn means that it is unlikely that we see any immediate bounce back in investment in UK automotive and manufacturing. It was noteworthy that Tesla CEO Elon Musk said recently that Brexit uncertainty was a factor in the firm's decision to build its first major European factory near Berlin in Germany rather than in the UK. [9]

The risks remain high. Peugeot has already stated this year that investment at Vauxhall at Ellesmere Port where the current Astra model is due to be replaced in 2021 is "contingent on the terms of the future trading relationship between the UK and the EU, and ensuring that PSA can make a profitable investment". [10] The firm is especially keen to see tariffs avoided, and has stressed that investment would be switched to Southern Europe in the event of no deal in particular (the merger with Fiat also gives it plenty of switching options); although where that leaves the plant in the event of a limited trade deal that just eliminates most tariffs is unclear. At the time of writing, some Astra production (the Astra estate) is being shifted to Germany and there is a sense that the clock is ticking for the plant. Nissan has given similar warnings over Qashqai production at Sunderland. [11]

Trade bodies representing manufacturing industries have expressed concern. Last autumn, aerospace, automotive, chemicals, food and drink and pharmaceutical industry bodies came together to warn the government that the kind of bare-bones trade relationship that the government appears to be aiming at in the political declaration was problematic for them and could pose a "serious risk to manufacturing competitiveness". [12]

Their letter stressed the need for regulatory alignment. These industries want to see such alignment in order to avoid customs checks. The point here is that customs essentially try to ensure that any differences between imported goods and domestic standards don't introduce risk to the market or the supply chain.[13] In simple terms, the more that standards and regulations vary across two countries, the more customs checks will take place on goods being traded between them.

So 'taking back control' means the ability for the UK to set new regulations and standards after Brexit but the knock-on effect will likely mean more customs checks and possible delays to, say, manufacturing components moving across borders, bringing challenges for manufacturers.

An agreement both formal and binding

A UK-EU trade agreement could of course remove barriers to trade by aligning regulations; the UK and EU could agree to share equivalent standards, or recognise that authorities in each can conduct approved checks, thereby ensuring that standards are met and allowing customs authorities to waive checks. But this would need a formal and binding agreement; simply aligning regulations informally would not cut it: checks would occur and goods crossing borders wouldn't receive the 'preferential treatment' needed to keep trade 'frictionless'.

The key point here is that manufacturing is highly exposed to the form of trade deal that is pursued. Mike Hawes, the chief executive of the Society of Motor Manufacturers and Traders (SMMT) has repeatedly stressed the needs of UK automotive[14] in this sense in terms of frictionless trade, with regulatory alignment[15] and continued access to talent, stressing that a close trading relationship is essential to unlock investment. That would essentially mean some sort of sectoral deal for automotive, but that would likely in turn mean the UK signing up to 'level playing field' provisions with the EU.

Even so, there are practical difficulties to be overcome with sectoral deals for industries like automotive. A free trade agreement (FTA) would make exported cars free of tariffs into the EU, but to benefit from this the cars need to meet 'rules of origin'. These require some 60 per cent of the value of a car's parts and components to be 'local' (that is from the UK) to benefit from the FTA and hence avoid tariffs, or for there to be a 'cumulation' agreement that counted parts from the UK and EU. [16]

So to eliminate border bureaucracy there would need to be an FTA arrangement and some sort of mutual recognition agreement for assessing conformity assessment (the process used to demonstrate that the product such as a car meets specified requirements). However, to ensure automatic mutual recognition of the UK's conformity assessment, European Economic

Area (EEA) states have to accept supranational enforcement. This could violate a UK 'red line' in Brexit talks.

One possibility would be to sign a special FTA agreement in which both sides agreed that in industries where the UK keeps the same external tariffs as the EU's common external tariff then rules of origin would not be checked. Such a deal is imaginable in cars as Holmes (2016) notes because both sides have an interest in maintaining the deeply entwined value chains across the sector. [17]

It should be stressed that simply sourcing more components in the UK isn't going to happen automatically either, given the barriers to 'reshoring' manufacturing we have identified in our own work in this area (see Bailey and De Propris, 2014[18]). That would require a much more supportive industrial policy than we have seen of late in the UK. Indeed whatever the form of Brexit, it seems that a better funded and more active industrial policy will be needed to boost competitiveness in the UK automotive sector and manufacturing more broadly.

In summary, exiting the EU in an orderly way with a trade deal and minimal trade friction beyond the transition period remains vital for UK manufacturing and the auto industry. While no deal at the end of 2020 would be highly damaging to output, jobs and investment, even a bare-bones trade agreement that just eliminates tariffs could still be costly for manufacturing to live with, given how tightly entwined manufacturing value chains are across the UK and EU.

Notes

1. https://www.smmt.co.uk/vehicle-data/car-registrations/
2. https://www.smmt.co.uk/vehicle-data/manufacturing/
3. UK hit by sharpest deterioration in manufacturing in 7 years, Financial Times, 2nd January 2020. https://www.ft.com/content/436b31c6-2d45-11ea-bc77-65e4aa615551
4. Supported by a £500m loan guarantee form the UK government: https://www.theguardian.com/business/2019/jul/15/jaguar-land-rover-offered-500m-loan-to-develop-electric-cars
5. Aston Martin SUV Production Launches in Wales, Wards Auto, 19th December 2019, https://www.wardsauto.com/industry/aston-martin-suv-production-launches-wales
6. Good news for the UK car industry could be undone by a no-deal Brexit, Daily Telegraph, 5th July 2019.

7. https://www.telegraph.co.uk/politics/2019/07/05/good-news-uk-car-industry-could-undone-no-deal-brexit/

8. See forecasts in 'Keeping the Wheels on the Road. UK Auto post Brexit' Bitesize Books (2019).

9. Automotive Brexit myths – busted, Society of Motor Manufacturers and Traders. https://www.smmt.co.uk/industry-topics/brexit/automotive-brexit-myths-busted/

10. Why Germany beat the UK to Tesla's European gigafactory, Daily Telegraph, 13th November 2019,

11. https://www.telegraph.co.uk/technology/2019/11/13/elon-musk-picked-germany-not-uk-teslas-europe-gigafactory/

12. Fears grow for Vauxhall's UK car plant with work being shifted to Germany, Daily Telegraph, 14th January 2020, https://www.telegraph.co.uk/business/2020/01/14/fears-grow-vauxhalls-uk-car-plant-work-shifted-germany/

13. Bailey, D (2019) Nissan's no deal warning is no surprise – but even a Johnson deal still offers challenges for UK auto, https://ukandeu.ac.uk/nissans-no-deal-warning-is-no-surprise-but-even-a-johnson-deal-still-offers-challenges-for-uk-auto/

14. Government faces industry backlash on Brexit plans, BBC News, 11th October 2019. https://www.bbc.co.uk/news/business-50019069

15. Institute for Government (2017) Implementing Brexit: Customs. https://www.telegraph.co.uk/technology/2019/11/13/elon-musk-picked-germany-not-uk-teslas-europe-gigafactory/

16. Bailey, D (2019) Auto industry issues stark new warning on no deal Brexit, https://ukandeu.ac.uk/auto-industry-issues-stark-new-warning-on-no-deal-brexit/

17. UK industry calls for tariff-free deal with EU as output slumps 17 per cent in Nov, Automotive News Europe, 20th December 2019, https://europe.autonews.com/automakers/uk-industry-calls-tariff-free-deal-eu-output-slumps-17-nov

18. UK assembled cars have far less local content on average. Some sort of 'cumulation agreement' and conformity of assessment will then be needed, in turn requiring international oversight.

19. Holmes, P (2016) A special deal for the car industry: how could it work? http://www.sussex.ac.uk/eu/articles/brexit-special-deal

20. Bailey, D and L De Propris (2014) Manufacturing reshoring and its limits: the UK automotive case, *Cambridge Journal of regions, Economy and Society*, 7(3) 379-395. https://academic.oup.com/cjres/article/7/3/379/2864041

About the contributor

David Bailey is Professor of Business Economics at the Birmingham Business School, University of Birmingham, UK and an ESRC *UK in a Changing Europe Senior Fellow*. He has written extensively on industrial and regional policy, especially in relation to manufacturing and the auto industry. He has been involved in a number of recent major projects including the Horizon2020 Rise project Makers where he led the work package on industrial policy. He is editor-in-chief of the journal *Regional Studies* and Chair of the *RSA Europe* think-tank and policy forum. David is a regular media commenter and newspaper columnist. Tweet him @dgbailey

Funding

The writing of this chapter has been supported via the Economic and Social Research Council's *UK in a Changing Europe* programme, Grant Reference: ES/T000848/1

Chapter 9

Challenging uncertainty: Automotive workers have not been bystanders to Brexit

Industrial uncertainty and 'Brexit fatigue' became the main feature of 2019, yet evidence from trade union Unite shows how car workers are not bystanders in challenging uncertainty and overcoming divides, say Steve Turner and Ben Norman

"The car industry's 'just-in-time' supply chains rely on fluid cross-Channel trade routes. 1,100 trucks filled with car parts cross seamlessly from EU into UK each day."

So tweeted Brexit Secretary Steve Barclay, concluding with the reassuring commitment: *"We need to start talks now."* Less reassuring than this revelation was its timing, August 2019, a little over two months before what became the government's failed Brexit deadline of October 31.[1]

By this point little more evidence was needed that Tory Brexiteers had closed their ears to the automotive sector. By its third year Brexit had descended into the soundbites, egos and arcane procedures which make up the three-ring circus of parliamentary politics in crisis. The industrial fallout for 800,000 workers across the automotive appeared to be chalked up as collateral damage or, seen through the eyes of its ideologues like Professor Patrick Minford, a price worth paying.

As the trade union for automotive workers in every assembly site and throughout every supply chain, Unite has been guided by the collective expertise of half a million manufacturing workers, uniquely placing us to take responsibility as the leading voice within the trade union movement on Brexit.

Politically, Unite campaigned tirelessly for a Brexit deal to include the fullest possible tariff-free, frictionless access to the single market, which we believe could be negotiated on the basis of firm commitments from the UK on non-regression of workers' rights and commitments to social, consumer and environmental standards. Such a deal would have secured the foundation of the UK automotive sector's success allowing for the transformative green industrial strategy both industry and Unite has called for in order for the sector to meet the challenges of the decades ahead.

Uncertainty was not short lived

Unite's primary focus is industrial. After all, when the political parlour games end and a final settlement is reached between the UK and the European Union with all that entails, the first place most people will experience it will be at work.

Reports from across automotive workplaces attest that rather than being a short-lived side effect of the political crisis, industrial uncertainty became Brexit's main feature. From Sunderland to Ellesmere Port, and from Swindon to Birmingham this is playing out in investment decisions and at the bargaining table; reaching a crescendo as the government threatened a reckless no-deal Brexit. This uncertainty will of course remain after January 31ʹ 2020 as the countdown clock resets for the yearlong 'transitional period' of trade talks.

In the teeth of this, Unite shop stewards have sought to restore certainty to members and their success has been tracked in new research based on interviews with frontline workplace reps across industries, supported by polling of 2,000 automotive workers.

The results, *Taking back control: Brexit in the Workplace*[2], revealed that Brexit uncertainty had affected almost all the interviewed reps, with 60 per cent reporting at least one workplace issue linked to Brexit. While 10 per cent reported a direct impact, such as a postponement of new investment, 34 per cent believed that their employer was making a virtue of a crisis to use Brexit opportunistically at the bargaining table.

This uncertainty fed into a deepening 'Brexit fatigue' across workplaces, which in turn exasperated divisions wrought by the referendum in 2016. Importantly, the research showed that 60 per cent of workplace reps have taken the initiative industrially to restore certainty, fend off any cases of opportunism and begin healing difficult political divisions.

With some employers, where collective bargaining is strong and relationships have developed, most notably in the automotive sector, this has meant using information and consultation agreements or European Works Councils to secure a seat at the table to participate in Brexit contingency planning or to use pay talks to negotiate commitments to protect working rights in collective agreements. With a (significant) minority of employers, this meant using the collective strength of the membership to face down opportunistic attacks on pay or our bargaining rights.

What are automotive workers saying?

The largest reported concerns of Unite automotive reps was overwhelmingly the impact on jobs caused by disruption to industry (46 per cent) followed by workers' rights (22 per cent), safety regulations (8 per cent) and the rise in racism (8 per cent). Behind all of this however, lurked the more existential threat of a no-deal Brexit.

"Immediately we'd go to WTO rules, so we're potentially looking at a 10 per cent hike on any tariffs … So, clearly that's going to impact on the members. So, are there potentially going to be job losses? Models being removed? We don't know; that's the uncertainty. But they'll have to pass the cost on somewhere. Our industry will be affected, whether it's internally or our suppliers."

> – Unite Convenor, Automotive Sector, North East, Yorkshire and Humberside

"I think in the long-term – because there's only Jaguar Land Rover who are a British-based company – companies like BMW, Toyota, Mini, the Japanese companies, will look to move out of the UK and relocate in Europe where they will be able to move parts around without any tariffs, whereas if they stay in the UK then obviously there's going to be an issue with tariffs. So, that would be my concern that a lot of the foreign nationals pull out, maybe not next year or the year after, but certainly in 5-10 years down the line."

> – Unite Senior Rep, Automotive Sector, West Midlands

Consistent with PMI data, stockpiling was reported across supply chain sites as industry braced for Brexit day. In this situation shop stewards sought to negotiate short-time working agreements that will cause both the members and the company as little disruption as possible.

For some reps, uncertainty overtook the forecast outcomes of Brexit itself as their main concern. The extension of Article 50 in October was seen by some as an extension of uncertainty, in some cases exacerbating rather than resolving issues for members at plant level. In some cases, reps reported prolonging delays to pay talks and vehicle investments as the political process dragged into the New Year.

Some reps went as far as to argue that prolonged uncertainty only increased pressures on industrial relations.

"I don't think the extension will change anything, so I wish they'd just got on with it whatever and we'd deal with whatever comes, at least then we'd know where we stood. But at the minute, although the company's not using it to batter us, they tell us lots of different scenarios and things we need to change: "pay is becoming an issue"; "Brexit will make us less competitive and we're struggling anyway"… So, although they're not battering us, they are giving subtle messages that they will be using it in the future."

> − Unite Deputy Convenor, Automotive Sector, North East, Yorkshire and Humberside

To complicate the picture, Unite stewards are more than aware of the wider issues being complicated by Brexit. In parallel to the uncertainty surrounding future investments and the related pressures on pay and industrial relations the industry faces the government's mishandling of diesel, the transition to electrification and international trade tensions.

"We had the Chief Executive over about two years ago, shortly after the referendum, and before the referendum the company had taken the decision to invest in the plant for new products. And when I spoke to him he said, "If we had known the result of Brexit then we wouldn't have invested the money that we did". So, those have been retrospective comments, but they've also said when we've gone into pay talks that "we can't progress your pay because of the uncertainty over JLR, Brexit, the slowdown in China etc etc". So, it's not being used as a single issue, but as one of several issues."

> − Unite Senior Rep, Automotive Sector, West Midlands

The mixed reactions to political events, such as extending Article 50 in October, were obviously linked to workers' differing political perspectives on Brexit. Some reported frustrations and deepening 'Brexit fatigue,' while others hoped it would pave the way for a second referendum. This evidences how the unfolding political crisis deepened workplace divisions.

The majority of interviewed Unite stewards (90 per cent) identified themselves as 'pro-Remain', yet when asked for their preferred Brexit outcome the greatest proportion (38 per cent) supported (or at least reluctantly accepted) leaving on the condition that a deal between the UK and EU is reached that meets Unite's tests. This was very closely followed by calls to stop Brexit via another public vote (36 per cent).

While no single outcome commanded a clear majority a separate polling of automotive workers revealed that 44 per cent wanted Brexit completed, either with a deal (20 per cent) or even without a deal (24 per cent). This 44 per cent included former Leave voters of which only a small percentage has changed their minds and those who continued to see themselves as Remain supporters but conditionally accepted leaving if the right settlement was reached.

In interviews both Leave supporters and Remainers reconciled to leaving articulated these conditions as frictionless trade institutionalised through a customs union coupled with safeguards for working rights and protections for migrant workers.

As 2019 progressed and the political crisis continued a clear rise of support was seen for both stopping Brexit entirely and for leaving without a deal, a deep expression of the 'Brexit fatigue' that percolated across the industry to exasperate political divides.

Working together to defend our industry

Faced with deepening political divides Unite stewards saw the need to proactively guard against Brexit fatigue deepening into fatalism that could undermine our industrial ability to recognise and respond to the impact of Brexit (or as one rep put it: *"you can't prepare for Armageddon!"*).

Across automotive and beyond frontline reps actively demonstrated the 'Unite premium' with 60 per cent taking some form of action to mitigate the industrial impact of Brexit. Of these, over a quarter (28 per cent) actively mobilised their members to secure an agreement with employers that either defended (16 per cent) or improved (12 per cent) existing pay and condition.

Trade unions have played an instrumental role in supporting the automotive sector in becoming the success story of UK manufacturing. Now, despite the perfect storm of political and industrial crisis that face us, Unite shop stewards remain resolute in confronting challenges as our members' face them. As one shop steward from a plant in the North West put it:

"That's why trade unions exist. We can't just turn it on and off depending on the political situation; it's got to be a permanent presence, that's always been my view."

Unite is under no illusions that as we progress through 2020 there will be no let up to the uncertainties facing automotive workers. Once outside the political framework of the European Union, the Johnson government's free trade agenda will find it impossible to reconcile contradictory tensions and demands, especially when Tory Brexit ideology confronts the cold reality of global trade wars. If the North American Free Trade Agreement (Nafta) and Ceta (the EU-Canada deal) are to be any precedent, tensions between sectors of the economy will be stoked and traded, all while the biggest questions over the future of the automotive industry remain unanswered.

Unite's commitment to the future of the automotive industry is undiminished. As our members will continue to show, when we achieve unity on the industrial questions through strong collective agreements and common purpose, we can campaign for a strong future for our industries and triumph over the politics of division in the workplace.

Notes

1. Steve Barclay, Twitter, (2019), https://twitter.com/SteveBarclay/status/1166765868891725825
2. Waterman, Norman, Earls, (2019) *Taking back control: Brexit in the Workplace The role of Unite in meeting the industrial impact of Brexit,* Unite the Union.

About the contributors

Steve Turner is the Assistant General Secretary of Unite the Union with responsibility for over half a million members across UK manufacturing. He is also the TUC General Council spokesperson for international issues. Ben Norman is the automotive sector research officer for Unite the Union, with responsibility for tracking the industrial impact of Brexit.

Chapter 10

Down and out down under? Auto lessons for post-Brexit Britain

There are some tough lessons to be learnt from the experiences of what was the Australian automotive sector, says Alex de Ruyter

Does the demise of the Australian domestic car industry in a free-trade environment offer any lessons as the UK formally exits the EU at 11pm GMT on January 31' 2020, and post-Brexit trade negotiations (at the time of writing in January 2020) continue to mean uncertainty for UK auto?

As the recent drama around Honda's announcement of shutting down its Swindon plant by 2021, with the anticipated loss of 3,500 jobs (and knock-on losses in the supply chain) has demonstrated, the future of UK auto is now highly uncertain as the prospect of exiting the EU customs union and single market at the end of 2020, for a looser 'free-trade' agreement, or even reversion to WTO status (the so-called de facto no deal) looms. This only adds to pressures facing the industry arising out of a shift from diesel to electric vehicles and a dramatic slowdown in demand from the all-important Chinese market (and similarly for other key markets), as show in Table 1.

Table 1: UK passenger vehicle exports (by value) for selected countries and EU 2016-2019.

Exports (£££)	2016	2017	2018	2019 (Jan-Nov)
US	6,438,582,347	6,705,672,816	7,281,466,714	7,182,112,597
China	3,432,052,946	4,216,256,709	3,512,636,717	2,447,116,727
Australia	745,175,015	933,180,679	587,237,036	446,016,793

Fiji	1,025,224	501,727	437,900	308,000
Solomon Islands	21,917	7,668	6,832	9,099
India	38,626,712	43,701,101	44,602,598	27,096,985
EU	12,504,946,045	13,109,451,239	11,488,032,888	10,933,860,884

Source: HMRC Overseas Trade Statistics.

I focus on the departure of Ford from the city of Geelong in the state of Victoria, given its primacy as a key employer for the city for much of the 20th century (but also comparing with the demise of Mitsubishi in Adelaide and Toyota in Melbourne), and look at what measures were put in place by government to try to foster economic diversification and regeneration.

At this point, dear reader, I must confess a personal interest as I am originally from Geelong and worked in the Ford Casting Plant (for a very brief period of time) knocking 'slag' off engine blocks, and my father also worked at the factory.

The start of a new sector

The Ford Motor Company of Australia was formed in 1925 and production commenced in Geelong in that year (with other sites following in Adelaide, Sydney, Brisbane and Fremantle), originally producing the famous Model T [1] Domestic production was a necessity to supply the Australian market, as the government had banned the import of luxury goods (including car bodies) in 1917 during the First World War in order to promote domestic industries – and provide new employment for its (horse-drawn) carriage-makers.

Here was a key example of the policy of protectionism that was typified by tariffs, which was to endure until the 1970s. Following the Second World War, expansion of the domestic industry in 1948 saw the emergence of the rival iconic Holden brand (an Australian subsidiary of General Motors, also known as GMH), which soon dominated the domestic market.

This prompted Ford to develop and produce an Australian version of the US-designed Falcon in 1960[2] (with successive models also designed in Australia from 1972 onwards), specifically adapted to cope with the (often) harsh Australian driving conditions.

The rivalry between these two US-owned subsidiaries (producing big cars with six-cylinder and eight-cylinder / V8 engines and petrol consumption to match) continued through the 1960s, 1970s and 1980s, with the Ford Falcon and the Holden Kingswood and then Commodore (an Australian equivalent of the Vauxhall Omega) vying to be Australia's most popular car (even spawning a popular 1970s' television sit-com *Kingswood Country* with the lead character's characteristic line to his son, "You're not touching the Kingswood!" [3]).

The Japanese make inroads

However the 1970s also saw more economical Japanese vehicles begin to make inroads into the Australian market (with Datsun, now known as Nissan, being an early pioneer) as import tariffs were lowered, with a particularly notable tariff cut of 25 per cent in 1973 by the then Whitlam Labor[4] government.

Fierce opposition from domestic producers (notably GMH, which stood down 5,000 workers in response) saw this cut reduced to 15 per cent but it was notable at the time that the industry, which at its peak employed 100,000 people, was seen as being characterised by:

> "*Too many producers with extensive operations in multiple states, resulting in product proliferation, scale inefficiencies, and components industries that were forced into exceptionally short production runs, together with excessive and costly parts inventories.*" [5]

This combined with the rising costs of fuel would erode the popularity of the large cars such as the Falcon that had underpinned the profitability of the US-owned subsidiaries in Australia.

Japanese companies, namely Toyota and Mitsubishi (which took over the Chrysler operations in Tonsley Park in Adelaide in 1981), of course, had started production in Australia. However, increased trade liberalisation in the 1980s and 1990s (under both Labor and Conservative governments) emphasised measures to promote industry 'competitiveness' (the 1984 Button Plan of phased tariff reductions epitomised this for steel and textiles as well as automotive[6]).

This, combined with the emergence of the more cost-competitive 'Asian Tiger' economies, would combine to undermine fatally the logic of domestic production in Australia as the new century dawned. Thus, car production in Australia peaked in the 1970s (475,000 in 1970, which ranked Australia tenth in the world at the time) and declined more or less from there on. [7]

Large-scale production ends

By May 2013, Ford had declared its intention to close down its remaining production plants at Geelong and Broadmeadows (in Melbourne), following a cumulative period of successive losses. This had been preceded by Mitsubishi's closure of its Adelaide plant in 2008. [8] And GMH (December 2013) and Toyota (February 2014) followed suit, By the end of 2017 a period of some 70 years of large-scale vehicle production in Australia had come to an end.

For Geelong, the ceasing of manufacturing was particularly painful as, prior to the closure of Ford, manufacturing had provided (in 2012) some 44 per cent of the city's output. [9] The company, not only directly in terms of its own workforce but also in terms of dependent SMEs in the supply chain, was the most significant employer of the city's workforce. Whilst the Federal Labor Government in 2013 had provided a package of assistance measures to facilitate adjustment totalling some A$66m, these measures were principally focused on retraining. [10] Subsequent efforts have seen some manufacturing return to the site of Ford's former Geelong operations plant in the form of wind turbine assembly by Danish firm Vestas:

> *"The VREH will involve investment of approximately A$3.5m and directly employ over 20 employees. The project will train hundreds of local staff in wind turbine maintenance and see wind turbine component assembly in Australia for the first time in over 10 years."* [11]

However, as noted, the number of staff directly employed is trivial (20 employees as at November 2019). Further expansion of such jobs is ultimately linked to 'greening' the economy and again, the role of the state is pivotal in this regard – for example, through the imposition of more stringent renewable energy-use targets.

In this context, the government of the State of Victoria recently legislated a target of 50 per cent of its electricity generation coming from renewable energy sources by 2030. [12] It remains to be seen whether this can fully compensate for the loss of vehicle manufacturing to the Geelong region. At a nation-wide level, manufacturing employment increased slightly between 2016-17 and 2017-18 (most recent data available), from 829,797 to 840,325 persons, but this still represents a significant decline from the million-plus employment levels of a decade earlier (Australian Bureau of Statistics).

The Australian experience hence points to the primacy of the state in fostering industrial policy and industrialisation. In this sense, the availability of abundant, cheap raw materials (a 'location-specific advantage' as economist John Dunning would have called it in his 'eclectic paradigm' of explaining foreign direct investment) combined with a protectionist state regime that offered incentives such as land packages meant domestic production was the only feasible way to supply the Australian market.

Proximity to a large domestic market is also an attraction for car producers. Australia did not have a large or integrated domestic market, being subject to a historical legacy of varying jurisdictions across the different states.

Furthermore, its trade liberalisation and integration policies with the Asia-Pacific meant that it made more economic sense for companies such as Ford and Toyota to now produce in the geographically proximate countries of Indonesia and Thailand and export complete vehicles to Australia (not helped by a mining boom in the 2000s that raised the value of the Australian dollar and eroded export competitiveness). As such, the Australian experience also points to the transformative role of the state (at various spatial levels) as a driver of the structural changes all too readily solely attributed to globalisation. [13]

The parallels for Britain

For the Brexiting Britain, the parallels are striking. Like Australia in its protectionist days, domestic production was feasible when the presence of external trade barriers acted as an inhibitor to exporting to the UK from a country of origin outside the EU; and the location-specific advantages of the UK with its flexible market environment *inside* the EU made it an attractive location to be a production platform integrated with the rest of the EU.

Also striking is how the car industry in the UK, much like Ford was in Geelong, is particularly important for middling-sized towns/cities such as Coventry, Wolverhampton, Derby and Swindon (all in areas with a majority Brexit vote).

Stripped of these advantages post-Brexit and facing likely new tariff and regulatory barriers, the clear incentive – as Honda and Nissan are currently demonstrating – for multinationals, will be to divest themselves over the coming period of production in the UK and reinvest elsewhere.

While state direction to foster the growth of high-technology sectors to compensate for the loss of vehicle production may soften the blow of plant closures and consequent job loss, the evidence to date suggests that the UK government has yet to learn the lessons of rapid task-force response to such events (with associated place-based industrial policy Australia at least has state governments that are forced to consider regional development as part of their *raison d'etre*) and the need to re-skill workers to compete in emergent sectors[14].

Epilogue

PS – I do not see anyone driving Falcons or Commodores anymore in Australia. Imported Japanese and European brands reign supreme...

Notes

1. https://www.abc.net.au/news/2016-10-07/timeline-ford-australia-ceases-production/7911742
2. https://www.abc.net.au/news/2016-10-07/timeline-ford-australia-ceases-production/7911742
3. http://www.adelaiderememberwhen.com.au/youre-not-touching-the-kingswood/
4. Labor, formally known as *the Australian Labor Party*, or ALP (American spelling convention used). The conservative parties in Australia have had various manifestations over the years, namely; *Free Trade Party, Nationalist Party, United Australia Party* and *Liberal Party*, generally as a coalition with the *Country Party* (now *National Party*).
5. http://theconversation.com/whitlam-made-the-case-for-reform-an-enduring-economic-legacy-33226
6. https://theconversation.com/whitlam-made-the-case-for-reform-an-enduring-economic-legacy-33226
7. https://en.wikipedia.org/wiki/Automotive_industry_in_Australia
8. See: Andrew Beer (2018), 'The closure of the Australian car manufacturing industry: redundancy, policy and community impacts', *Australian Geographer*, DOI: 10.1080/00049182.2017.1402452
9. https://www.thegordon.edu.au/sitedocs/skilling-the-bay/geelong-regional-labour-market-snapshot.aspx
10. https://www.abc.net.au/news/2016-10-07/timeline-ford-australia-ceases-production/7911742

11. https://www.rdv.vic.gov.au/news/wind-turbines-bring-manufacturing-jobs-to-geelong
12. https://www.cleanenergycouncil.org.au/news/wind-turbine-factory-brings-fresh-air-to-manufacturing-to-geelong
13. Ibid. Beer argues convincingly that this process has been typified by the Federal Government in Australia prioritising overall growth and competitiveness over regional well-being, with state governments and local authorities being left to deal with the "negative consequences of economic change".
14. See Bailey in this volume.

About the contributor

Professor Alex De Ruyter is Director at the Centre for Brexit Studies at Birmingham City University and is a co-editor of this book.

Bite-Sized Public Affairs Books are designed to provide insights and stimulating ideas that affect us all in, for example, journalism, social policy, education, government and politics.

They are deliberately short, easy to read, and authoritative books written by people who are either on the front line or who are informed observers. They are designed to stimulate discussion, thought and innovation in all areas of public affairs. They are all firmly based on personal experience and direct involvement and engagement.

The most successful people all share an ability to focus on what really matters, keeping things simple and understandable. When we are faced with a new challenge most of us need quick guidance on what matters most, from people who have been there before and who can show us where to start. As Stephen Covey famously said, "The main thing is to keep the main thing, the main thing."

But what exactly is the main thing?

Bite-Sized books were conceived to help answer precisely that question crisply and quickly and, of course, be engaging to read, written by people who are experienced and successful in their field.

The brief? Distil the 'main things' into a book that can be read by an intelligent non-expert comfortably in around 60 minutes. Make sure the book enables the reader with specific tools, ideas and plenty of examples drawn from real life. Be a virtual mentor.

We have avoided jargon – or explained it where we have used it as a shorthand – and made few assumptions about the reader, except that they are literate and numerate, involved in understanding social policy, and that they can adapt and use what we suggest to suit their own, individual purposes. Most of all the books are focused on understanding and exploiting the changes that we witness every day but which come at us in what seems an incoherent stream.

They can be read straight through at one easy sitting and then referred to as necessary – a trusted repository of hard-won experience.

Bite-Sized Books Catalogue

Don Sharp
Nothing Happens Until You Sell Something
A Personal View of Selling Techniques

Lifestyle Books

Anna Corthout
Alive Again
My Journey to Recovery
Anna Corthout
Mijn Leven Herpakt
Kruistocht naar herstel
Paul Davies – (Editor)
Still Crazy About George Eliot After 200 Years
A Joyful Celebration of Her Works and Novels
Phil Davies
Don't Worry Be Happy
A Personal Journey
Phil Davies
Feel the Fear and Pack Anyway
Around the World in 284 Days
Stuart Haining
My Other Car is an Aston
A Practical Guide to Ownership and Other Excuses to Quit
Work and Start a Business
Bill Heine
Cancer – Living Behind Enemy Lines Without a Map
Regina Kerschbaumer
Yoga Coffee and a Glass of Wine
A Yoga Journey
Gillian Perry
Capturing the Celestial Lights
A Practical Guide to Imagining the Northern Lights
Arthur Worrell
A Grandfather's Story
Arthur Worrell's War

Public Affairs Books

Eben Black
> Lies Lobbying and Lunch
>> PR, Public Affairs and Political Engagement – A Guide

John Mair and Richard Keeble (Editors)
> Investigative Journalism Today:
>> Speaking Truth to Power

John Mair, Richard Keeble and Farrukh Dhondy (Editors)
> V.S Naipaul:
>> The legacy

Christian Wolmar
> Wolmar for London
>> Creating a Grassroots Campaign in a Digital Age

John Mair and Neil Fowler (Editors)
> Do They Mean Us – Brexit Book 1
>> The Foreign Correspondents' View of the British Brexit

John Mair and Neil Fowler (Editors)
> Oil Dorado
>> Guyana's Black Gold

Sir John Redwood
> We Don't Believe You
>> Why Populists and the Establishment see the world
>> differently

John Mills
> Economic Growth Post Brexit
>> How the UK should Take on the World

Fiction

Paul Davies
> The Ways We Live Now
>> Civil Service Corruption, Wilful Blindness, Commercial
>> Fraud, and Personal Greed – a Novel of Our Times

Paul Davies
> Coming To
>> A Novel of Self-Realisation

Children's Books

Chris Reeve – illustrations by Mike Tingle
> The Dictionary Boy
>> A Salutary Tale

Fredrik Payedar
> The Spirit of Chaos
>> It Begins

Printed in Great Britain
by Amazon

14735711R00058